IMPEACH

Neal Katyal is the Paul and Patricia Saunders Professor of Law at Georgetown University, Washington, D.C., and a partner at a law firm where he leads one of the largest Supreme Court practices in the US. He previously served as Acting Solicitor General of the United States (the government's top courtroom lawyer). He has argued more Supreme Court cases in US history than has any minority attorney (39 in total). A frequent contributor to the *New York Times*, he has been named one of GQ's Men of the Year and has appeared on *House of Cards*, where he played himself.

Sam Koppelman is a senior speechwriter at Fenway Strategies, where he's written for public officials, philanthropists, business leaders and organisations working to make the world a better place. He has also been a speechwriter to former New York City Mayor Michael Bloomberg, and has written for publications including *Time* magazine and the *Washington Post*.

IMPEACH

THE CASE

AGAINST

DONALD

TRUMP

NEAL KATYAL

WITH SAM KOPPELMAN

CANONGATE

First published in Great Britain in 2019
by Canongate Books Ltd, 14 High Street, Edinburgh EH1 1TE

canongate.co.uk

Published in the USA in 2019 by Houghton Mifflin Harcourt
Publishing Company,
3 Park Avenue, 19th Floor, New York, NY 10016

1

British Library Cataloguing-in-Publication Data
A catalogue record for this book is available on
request from the British Library

ISBN 978 1 83885 212 2

Printed and bound in Australia by McPhersons Printing Group

Shall any man be above Justice? Above all shall that man be above it, who can commit the most extensive injustice? . . . Shall the man who has practised corruption and by that means procured his appointment in the first instance, be suffered to escape punishment, by repeating his guilt?

— GEORGE MASON, CONSTITUTIONAL
  CONVENTION, JULY 20, 1787

Against the insidious wiles of foreign influence . . . the jealousy of a free people ought to be constantly awake, since history and experience prove that foreign influence is one of the most baneful foes of republican government.

— GEORGE WASHINGTON, FAREWELL ADDRESS,
  SEPTEMBER 19, 1796

This business of high crimes and misdemeanors goes to the question of whether or not the person serving as President of the United States put their own interests, their personal interests, ahead of public service.

— MICHAEL PENCE, HOUSE OF REPRESENTATIVES,
  JULY 25, 2008

Contents

Introduction

I magine if it had worked.

Imagine if our president had leveraged his role as commander in chief to convince a foreign power to open an investigation into his political opponent.

Imagine if the president's rival lost the primary because news broke that he was under investigation.

Imagine if that meant the president faced a weaker candidate in November 2020 — and won reelection as a result.

Imagine if our president owed his victory to a foreign power and we never found out.

Imagine how much leverage the leaders of that country would have on our foreign policy decisions.

Imagine how easily they could blackmail our commander in chief.

Imagine what our president would do next, knowing he could subvert our democracy without paying a price.

Now, imagine if, eventually, we did find out. But it was too late — because he had already won.

Imagine if our president abused the power vested in him to win — and we knew it.

Imagine what that would do to our faith in elections, to our trust in government, to our belief that we live in a democracy.

If President Trump's efforts to coerce Ukraine into interfering with our democracy had stayed a secret until the 2020 election — if a brave whistleblower hadn't risked his career, and his safety, to speak out — we would have fundamentally, perhaps irrevocably, lost faith in the legitimacy of our republic.

That is why we have no choice but to impeach and remove President Trump: because he wielded the powers of the presidency to serve himself instead of the people he represents; because he was willing to undermine our democracy to help his prospects of reelection; and because he has stated, repeatedly and unapologetically, that he would do it again.

"A Grave and Sobering Decision"

Five minutes and 21 seconds after 7 p.m. on July 27, 1974, by a vote of 27 to 11, the House Judiciary Committee made Richard Nixon the first president since 1868 to be formally accused of an impeachable offense. The vote came more than two years after James McCord, Virgilio Gonzales, Frank Sturgis, Eugenio Martinez, and Bernard Barker broke into the Watergate building in Washington, DC. So one might imagine that after months of stonewalling, lying, and deceit from the Nixon Administration, Democrats on the committee would have felt a bit of catharsis on that July night. But they felt no such thing.

In a *Washington Post* article dated the next day — headlined "Judiciary Committee Approves Article to Impeach President,

27–11: 6 Republicans Join Democrats to Pass Obstruction Charge" — Democratic members of the House didn't express jubilance, but sorrow. Representative Paul Sarbanes, who helped run the floor debate, said his vote had been "a grave and sobering decision." As the *Post* wrote, "Even those whose impeachment votes were never in doubt voiced no sense of triumph."

"I don't want to talk to anybody," said Democratic representative Barbara Jordan from Texas. Democrat Charles Rangel from New York cried, "It's a terrible thing to happen to anybody." And Chairman Peter Rodino, another Democrat, simply stated, "I'm not happy."

Representative Walter Flowers, a Democrat from Alabama, who had been one of the last holdouts on impeachment, said he came to his conclusion only after spending weeks studying the facts of the case and the Constitution of the United States. "It is clear to me what I must do," he said, but he worried that his constituents would be upset by his vote. His consolation? "I probably have enough pain for both them and me."

This is impeachment in the United States of America — a most extraordinary measure, reserved only for the rare occasions when a president proves himself unable or unwilling to serve the interests of the people he represents. Nobody involved in impeachment proceedings leaves them unscathed. And every time our nation even considers reversing the lawful election of a president, we lose a piece of our democracy. But when our founders wrote the Constitution, they knew there would be times when our democracy would be even more damaged if we failed to impeach our president.

All 27 members of the House Judiciary Committee who voted to impeach Nixon recognized this. They may have done so with heavy hearts, but they also had peace of mind—because they knew the Constitution had left them with no choice but to remove him.

That, I believe, is where America finds itself today.

Why I Wrote This Book

In 2016, America elected Donald Trump to be its 45th president. That means all of us, even those who disagree with his policies, have a duty to recognize him as our commander in chief. I certainly do.

I am not a partisan.

I'm a lawyer who has argued more United States Supreme Court cases than just about anyone (39 and counting) and convinced everyone from Justice Scalia to Justice Ginsburg to side with my clients, who have ranged from death-penalty defendants to the largest companies in the world to the most recent national-security whistleblower to take his case to the Supreme Court. I have also been a law professor for more than two decades at Georgetown University, where I have taught impeachment twenty times (and even once taught a semester-long class called "Clinton" about all the legal issues his presidency presented). As Acting Solicitor General of the United States, I served as President Obama's top courtroom lawyer for a time, representing the US government in the highest court in the land.

But I am also what I call an extremist centrist.

What does that mean? It means I try to find wisdom in all sorts of places and don't disagree with Republicans on everything—not even with President Trump. In fact, I formally introduced President Trump's first nominee to the Supreme Court,

Neil Gorsuch, to the US Senate at his confirmation hearings, just days after I filed a lawsuit challenging the president's Muslim ban. Justice Gorsuch wasn't my friend, but I had seen him in court many times and knew he would continue to be a real judge. Many Democrats were furious with me. But I respected him, and I remembered how frustrated I felt when Republicans voted against Elena Kagan, who couldn't have been more qualified. I wanted Democrats to apply the same yardstick to Justice Gorsuch that I felt Republicans should have applied to Justice Kagan.

I live my life by this Yardstick Rule, because the only way to preserve the rule of law is to apply the same standards to everyone, regardless of whether or not you agree with their views. That's how I teach my law students: I ask them which side they are more sympathetic to in a trial and then make them represent the other party to the case. So if they like the plaintiff's argument, I have them pretend they're the defendant's lawyer; and vice versa. This approach is rooted in all sorts of fancy philosophical terms, like John Rawls's "veil of ignorance," but the central idea is simple: the shoe is going to be on the other foot one day. Being able to recognize that is the definition of principle, and for me, it's principle over party every day of the week.

This is why I believe Congress should exercise extreme caution before impeaching a president. In a democracy, we have no responsibility more sacred than respecting the will of the people, and if Democrats impeach a duly elected Republican for purely partisan reasons today, then Republicans can push to do the same to a Democrat tomorrow.

Our founders placed such a high bar on removing a president for this very reason. And Congress has indeed chosen to reserve impeachment only for the extreme circumstances in which our representatives believe a president has committed treason, brib-ery, or other high crimes and misdemeanors.

Only two presidents in our nation's history — Andrew Johnson and Bill Clinton — have been impeached by the House of Repre-sentatives, and neither was convicted by the Senate. (Nixon, un-derstanding he faced almost certain removal from office, resigned before the House could formally bring charges against him.) Only 19 officials in total have been impeached by the House since 1797, when William Blount, a senator from Tennessee, became the first. For a sense of how long ago that was, consider that Blount was impeached for helping Great Britain seize the land that's now Florida and Louisiana . . . from Spain.

The rarity of impeachments, particularly presidential ones, underscores a simple truth: in ordinary times, even when Con-gress has disagreed with a president's policies, demeanor, or con-duct, our representatives have recognized the legitimacy of who-ever the American people elect.

But we live in a time with a president who is far from ordi-nary. And while our founders believed impeachment should be an option of last resort, they put it in the Constitution to make it available when needed, not to serve as a hollow adornment.

As James Madison wrote in *Federalist No. 51*, "If men were angels, no government would be necessary." Alas, men — and women and everyone else — aren't all angels, including, perhaps even especially, our elected officials. That's why Madison went on to say, "In framing a government which is to be administered by men over men, the great difficulty lies in this: You must first enable the government to control the governed; and in the next place oblige it to control itself."

Our Constitution is filled with mechanisms by which the government can, to borrow Madison's term, "control itself." These include federalism, which distributes responsibilities between states and the federal government; separation of powers, which ensures that the executive, legislative, and judicial branches can serve as checks on one another; and, of course, impeachment, which provides Congress with the ability to remove a president from office.

The standards for impeachment are high, but they are not impossible to meet. If a majority of the House votes to charge the president with a high crime (this is called "impeachment") and two-thirds of the Senate rules him guilty (this is called "conviction" or "removal"), then he has no choice but to step down. Of course, convincing 67 out of 100 senators to agree on something is no small task, which is why only eight officials have ever been removed from office by the Senate. And there's reason to believe it will be especially hard today, at a time when senators from different parties can hardly be convinced to talk to one another, let alone vote for the same bill.

But at the darkest moments in American history, the hearts and minds of Americans have proven to be far stronger than party politics. With pressure from constituents, Congress could still very well put country over party and impeach President Trump. And I hope that a book like this, which outlines what President Trump did, when he did it, and why it meets the Constitution's standards for impeachment, can help build that pressure.

I believe this because at bottom our Constitution, and indeed the entire American experiment, is all about protecting our democracy from threats like these; and because all of America's most influential thinkers, from across the political spectrum—

from Antonin Scalia to George Washington to Barack Obama—have shared a belief that our democracy can be sustained only if ours remains a government of laws, not of men.

That's why I'm writing to you: the American people. You're not my normal audience, which is a court of law, but only if you speak up can the judge and jury in this case, Congress, rule guilty.

Why We Can't Wait Until the Next Election

I recognize why Americans from both political parties are so wary of impeachment. Republicans are rightly frustrated by the idea of removing a president whose policies they generally support. And Democrats are understandably afraid of the blowback they'll receive from taking so drastic a step.

In many ways, both political parties would be better off if President Trump's fate were determined on Election Day. But the challenge we face is this: President Trump has shown that he will do everything in his power, legal and illegal, to ensure he wins reelection, even if that means working with a foreign power to undermine our democracy. So asking us to wait until the election to remove him from office is like asking to resolve a dispute based on who wins a game of Monopoly—when the very crime you've been accused of is cheating at Monopoly.

That's the problem: we can't decide President Trump's fate with the 2020 election because there's no guarantee he won't try again to use the powers vested in him to rig it. And that, in turn, means that if we want to save our country before it's too late, he has left us with no choice but to impeach him now.

Why Our Founders (and Vice President Pence) Would Have Impeached President Trump

Our founders predicted we would face a moment like this. When they wrote about removing a president for "high crimes and misdemeanors," they were thinking first and foremost of a commander in chief who wielded the powers of the presidency for the benefit of himself instead of for the benefit of the people. As Alexander Hamilton wrote in *Federalist No. 65*, our framers wanted to protect America from "those offenses which proceed from . . . the abuse or violation of some public trust." And there was no such "abuse of trust" they were more afraid of than foreign interference.

In one of the greatest speeches ever given by a president, George Washington, our first commander in chief, delivered a farewell address that called foreign influence over our political system "one of the most baneful foes of republican government." Similarly, John Adams believed that "the danger of foreign Influence" would "recur" as "often as elections happen." And when James Madison proposed including impeachment in our Constitution, he said he did so in part to ensure no president would "betray his trust to foreign powers."

Why did our founders decide that being beholden to a foreign power was an impeachable offense? Because, as Hamilton said, a president should answer only to the American people. That means never abusing the office for personal gain — or to serve the interests of a foreign power.

In 2008, a congressman captured this point well during a hearing at the House Judiciary Committee. "This business of high crimes and misdemeanors," he said, referencing a witness's report, "goes to the question of whether or not the person serving as President of the United States put their own interests, their personal interests, ahead of public service." The congressman who said that? None other than Mike Pence, now President Trump's vice president.

Over the course of this book, I'll revisit the "Pence Standard," because Vice President Pence's quote perfectly distills why our founders believed Congress has an obligation to hold accountable a president who abuses the power of his office — a president, in other words, like Donald Trump.

Why We Need to Impeach President Trump (and Why This Is Different from Mueller)

I know you've heard some of this before. Over President Trump's first two years in office, Democrats spent almost every day discussing Russia. They called President Trump an asset, a spy, a traitor. They said Special Counsel Robert Mueller would produce the evidence necessary to impeach and remove President Trump. And, in the end, they were wrong: Mueller's report did not lead to President Trump's removal.

There's no denying that Mueller's investigation was conducted professionally, by some of America's finest lawyers. The report they produced found striking instances of obstruction of justice. And many respected legal minds believe Mueller's report, in and of itself, provided enough evidence to impeach President Trump.

But if you weren't convinced by Mueller's report, if you believe President Trump's actions in 2016 did not warrant impeachment, then this book is for you. Because the proven facts of what President Trump has done with Ukraine far eclipse the allegations of his campaign's coordination with Russia in 2016.

Whereas Mueller's report could not prove collusion, in this case there is no doubt President Trump tried to collude with President Volodymyr Zelensky of Ukraine — because we have notes from the call, released by President Trump himself, demonstrating our president doing exactly that.

Whereas much of Mueller's report focused predominantly on President Trump's conduct prior to taking office (which meant he wasn't beholden to the Pence Standard), the Ukraine scandal is about the actions Donald Trump has taken *as president,* our most powerful official.

Why is that distinction important? Well, in 2016, Trump had to look up to the sky and ask Russia to hack Secretary Clinton's emails without having anything specific to offer in return (so far as we know, anyway). In 2019, by contrast, with the full imprimatur of being our head of state and with millions of dollars in military aid to withhold or dole out, he called up the president of Ukraine directly and made the request for him to interfere in our elections — knowing he could use the power of the purse of the United States as leverage.

What's more, whereas Mueller's report didn't contain any smoking-gun evidence of coordination between Trump and Russia, we have concrete evidence of President Trump asking Ukraine to do him a "favor" in exchange for help procuring weapons.

And we have a transcript of a text from Bill Taylor, the top US diplomat to Ukraine, saying that "it's crazy to withhold security assistance for help with a political campaign," as well as testimony from Ambassador Taylor confirming that this is what Trump was doing. Acting White House chief of staff Mick Mulvaney went so far as to admit from the White House briefing room that there

was a quid pro quo ("something for something") exchange between President Trump and President Zelensky—before eventually trying to walk it back. And while you'll soon learn that a
quid pro quo is not necessary at all for impeachment, there's no
doubt that President Trump's blatant solicitation of a bribe adds
to the case for his impeachment, in a way nothing in the Mueller
report ever did.

Moreover, not only do we have transcripts of, texts about, and
witnesses to the president's most recent crimes—including Lt.
Col. Alexander S. Vindman, who heard the call himself—but we
also have repeated confessions from the president himself in the
public record. Whereas he cried "no collusion" throughout Special Counsel Mueller's investigation, President Trump is issuing
no such denials about Ukraine. "I have an absolute right," he has
tweeted, "to investigate, or have investigated, CORRUPTION,
and that would include asking, or suggesting, other Countries to
help us out!"

President Trump knows there's no hiding his coordination
with Ukraine—so instead of denying it, he's defending it. And
he's doubling down, asking China to join Ukraine in investigating Vice President Biden as well. That's because President Trump
believes his best strategy for surviving this scandal is to pretend
it's not a big deal, and he's betting that his supporters will go along
with his story.

This is the approach of a man who believes he "could stand in
the middle of Fifth Avenue and shoot somebody" without losing
any voters. The question is whether he's right—whether Americans will be too blinded by partisanship to see what President
Trump has done. Or to care.

That could very well be the case, but I wrote this book because
I am not ready to give up on the American people; and because

I believe that if we fail to hold President Trump accountable for what he did in 2019 — for what he's doing *right now* — we might lose our democracy altogether in 2020.

That's not only because I worry about foreign influence on our elections; it's also because I am afraid of the standard we would set for future presidents if we fail to impeach this one. If we allow President Trump to commit a paradigmatic impeachable offense — one of the very high crimes our Constitution was designed to prevent — then we will set a precedent that our commander in chief cannot be held accountable. And in a world where the Constitution makes the president all-powerful — in charge of the world's largest treasury and the world's strongest army — an unconstrained presidency is a constitutional monstrosity.

As Edmund Randolph said at the Constitutional Convention, "The Executive will have great opportunities of abusing his power." One of the only ways for him to be stopped, the founders understood, was through removal — which means that if impeachment is effectively written out of our Constitution (as Trump's lawyers have urged), the president of the United States will effectively be above the law.

To crystallize this point: if Congress does not impeach President Trump, President Nixon's infamous answer to David Frost — "When the president does it, that means that it is not illegal" — will transform from being a much-derided overstatement of executive power to being a statement of fact. Not only will future presidents feel emboldened to invite foreign influence into our democracy, they will believe they can commit any crime at all — even (or especially) one that helps them get reelected. And if the precedent set by the failure to impeach Trump is any indication, they will be right.

That is a price all of us — Republicans and Independents and Democrats alike — must be unwilling to pay.

Why You Should Read This Book

I also wrote this book because impeachment isn't meant to be conducted solely in late-night meetings on Capitol Hill, in war room discussions around the Resolute desk, or in overnight strategy sessions at DC law firms.

Yes, the House will ultimately vote on impeachment and the Senate will vote on removal, but in America, our elected officials don't represent themselves. They represent the people. And the only way they will be courageous enough to impeach President Trump is if their constituents demand they perform their duty as a check on the executive branch and remove him from office.

Now, I don't want you to simply take my word on whether the president has committed a high crime. My goal with this book isn't to convince you that President Trump should be impeached, though I do make the case. It's to provide you with the information you need to decide for yourself.

All I ask is that you apply the same yardstick to President Trump that you would to President Obama. As I mentioned earlier, I call this the Yardstick Rule, and it's really simple: you just ask yourself, in a moment of brutal honesty, what you would do if the political parties were reversed. Just close your eyes and imagine President Obama had done what President Trump did — if he'd asked Iran, for instance, to dig up dirt on Mitt Romney. If you are a Democrat, would you have supported impeachment? If you are a Republican, would you?

Over the course of this book, I will provide you with all the facts you need to make that determination — not only about President Trump and Ukraine but about the history of impeachment: about why it was included in our Constitution, how it has been enforced throughout our history, and where all of that leaves us today.

Of course, new information may very well be revealed between when this book was written and when you read it, but the story told here, with the facts already at our disposal, is all you need to decide for yourself whether or not President Trump should be impeached. It doesn't matter why military aid was withheld for a time. It doesn't matter whether Ukraine did in fact open up an investigation into Hunter Biden. All that matters is that President Trump asked for Ukraine's help in compromising a political rival, without the American public knowing about it. My answers to the other questions, like whether there was a quid pro quo (there was) and whether there was a cover-up (there was), are gravy. The central issue here is the one we've known about since September 2019: President Trump's solicitation of election interference from a foreign power.

So keep your eye on the ball and don't get distracted by sideshows. Impeaching a president, by design, is hard. It will require the unwavering focus of the American people. This book is designed to show you what to focus on and what questions to ask.

In Chapter 1, I discuss the origins of impeachment: why our founders included it in our Constitution, how it's defined, and when it's been used against past presidents. In Chapter 2, I examine the evidence available to us with regard to President Trump's conduct with Ukraine, and in Chapter 3, I explain why I believe the only viable remedy is impeachment. In Chapter 4, I answer some of the most commonly asked questions about impeachment, from how it works (it's complicated) to how long it takes (it depends) — and respond to the most common defenses of President Trump's actions. And in Chapter 5, I contemplate what America would look like after the impeachment of President Trump and what laws we could pass to ensure that no president can abuse their power in the same way again.

Ultimately, I believe that America will not be saved by our Constitution, or our laws, or even our elected officials. If our country survives this crisis, it will be because of Americans like you, Americans who remember that our government is meant to be of, by, and for the people — and stand up to declare that no one is above the law.

Not even the president of the United States.

A BRIEF HISTORY OF IMPEACHMENT

The case against President Trump did not begin when he asked Ukrainian president Zelensky to do him a favor in 2019.

No, the case against President Trump began long before he ever took the oath of office; long before he decided to run for president; long before he was born.

The case against President Trump began at the very founding of our country — when 56 colonists came together to declare they would never again be ruled by an executive with unchecked power. To be exact: The case against President Trump began on July 4th, 1776.

That Time We Impeached King George III

Decades before Congress filed the first articles of impeachment, our founders drafted the Declaration of Independence.

The Declaration is remembered today for its opening lines — about self-evident truths, about all men being created equal, about life, liberty, and the pursuit of happiness. Children memorize these paragraphs in elementary school classrooms. Civil rights leaders, marching for liberty, have invoked them throughout our history. Politicians across our country, from every party, wax poetic about those opening words.

And yet — few could tell you what comes next.

After the soaring rhetoric in its opening lines, the Declaration of Independence transitions into a list of "repeated injuries and usurpations" caused by Britain's King George III. The first one is haunting: "He has refused his Assent to Laws, the most wholesome and necessary for the public good." And so are the 26 additional offenses our founders delineate, ranging from "[obstructing] the Administration of Justice" to "[refusing] to cause others to be elected."

"A Prince whose character is thus marked by every act which may define a Tyrant," the signers conclude, "is unfit to be the ruler of free people." No longer, they declared, would they bow to King George III, because the United States would be, from that moment onward, "Free and Independent."

In this way, the Declaration amounts to what could be considered America's first articles of impeachment. So it's no surprise that when it came time for our founders to write a constitution of their own, one of their central objectives was ensuring that our country would never be ruled by someone asserting kinglike powers again. As Benjamin Franklin explained, referring to George Washington, "The first man put at the helm will be a good one." But, he added, "Nobody knows what sort may come afterwards." "The executive will be always increasing here, as elsewhere," he warned, "till it ends in a monarchy."

That belief, shared among our founders, is the reason they included so many checks and balances on presidential powers and prerogatives in our Constitution. It's why, in the Constitution's *first* article, they created Congress — so the legislative branch could check the executive, whose creation came only later, in Article II. It's why they split Congress into two chambers, the House of Representatives and the Senate, so no one body would have too much power. And, to create what James Madison called a "double security," it's also why they divided power between the central government and states.

Our founders' fear of any individual person having too much power also led to the establishment of judicial review — and to fixed terms of office, which ensured that the president of the United States would be subject to elections every four years, instead of being granted open-ended government service.

Every single one of these checks and balances was designed, at least in part, to prevent America from devolving into the very kind of monarchical government from which our country declared its independence. But in the summer of 1787, our founders realized that even these checks were not enough — because any president could simply decide to ignore them. That meant our country needed another tool to hold our president accountable: impeachment.

The Constitutional Convention

The Constitutional Convention began in May, but the question of impeachment didn't come into focus until two months later — on July 20, 1787. On that hot summer day, two of the convention's delegates, Charles Pinckney and Gouverneur Morris, laid out the case against Congress having the power to remove a president from office. Their belief was simple: If a president were so bad, wouldn't he simply lose his next election? Why, they asked, would you ever need to preempt the will of the people?

These were important questions, but Charles and Gouverneur's fellow delegates had answers. George Mason in particular had a knack for tearing down any arguments opposing impeachment. "Shall any man be above justice?" he exclaimed. "Above all shall that man be above it, who can commit the most extensive injustice? . . . Shall the man who has practised corruption & by that means procured his appointment in the first instance," he concluded, "be suffered to escape punishment, by repeating his guilt?"

In other words, without the protection of impeachment, what would stop a president from committing crimes to win office — particularly if he knew that he would have full immunity afterward?

Mason sometimes operated as a one-man idea factory, but he had supporters this time. Here, crucially, James Madison, a chief architect of the Constitution, agreed with him on the floor of the convention. The president, Madison warned, "might lose his capacity after his appointment. He might pervert his administration into a scheme of [embezzlement] or oppression." Or, he added, in words with special resonance today, "he might betray his trust to foreign powers." Only impeachment, he believed, could protect our country from a president guilty of offenses like these.

William Richardson Davie, from North Carolina, made a similar point, warning that an unimpeachable president might just "spare no efforts or means whatever to get himself reelected."

The debate went on for a while. Rufus King, a delegate from Massachusetts, was left unconvinced by Madison's argument. As historian Jill Lepore writes, King, like Morris, "worried that the independence of the executive branch would be lost if the threat of impeachment were wielded by the legislative branch and held over the President."

But while King had a point, the delegates were ultimately more receptive to an argument made by Elbridge Gerry. "A good magistrate will not fear [Congress]," Gerry said. "A bad one ought to be kept in fear of them."

At one point, as tensions grew between those who supported impeachment and those who did not, Benjamin Franklin, whose remarks often carried more weight than those of anyone else present, quieted the room. "What was the practice before this in cases where the chief Magistrate rendered himself obnoxious?" Franklin asked, before providing a chilling and brief answer to his own question: "Assassination."

· While Franklin understood impeachment could be burdensome, he believed that a legal mechanism for removing a public official was all that stood between our democracy devolving into anarchy the moment a president was deemed by the people to be unfit for office.

By the end of the day, Gerry, Madison, Mason, and Franklin had convinced the majority of the convention that impeachment should in fact be included in the Constitution. As Lepore writes, "Even Gouverneur Morris had come around and changed his mind." In America, Morris concluded, "The people are the king." And so no one, not even our president, would be above the law.

How Impeachment Would Work

Over the following months, as the delegates determined how impeachment would work, they turned to an unlikely source for inspiration: the British.

The king of England, of course, could never be impeached, but Parliament did have a protocol for removing his ministers: the House of Commons was responsible for accusing officials, and then the House of Lords was responsible for trying them. While our founders were no fans of the British government, they thought this system worked well, so they devised a similar procedure for the United States.

The House of Representatives would investigate, and if the majority of the body agreed with charging the president, they would send articles of impeachment to the Senate, where the president would be tried. Only if two-thirds of the Senate agreed that a president's conduct was impeachable would he be removed from office. (As in criminal courts, the idea here is that the bar for conviction should be higher than the bar for indictment.)

The division of powers when it came to impeachment, our founders felt, was important, because the two halves of the legislature were designed to work differently from one another. Members of the House, they believed, would more directly represent the people they served, while senators would represent their states. (Before the 17th Amendment, ratified in 1913, senators were selected by state legislatures, not the people.) This structural dichotomy between House and Senate is the basis of Article I, Section 7 of the Constitution, which says that laws can be passed only if both Houses of Congress consent. (Even if 100 senators voted for a bill, it could never become law unless the House supported it too.) And a similar idea, based on Britain's bicameral legislative structure, undergirded their "two to tango" requirement for impeachment.

The founders' approach to impeachment, however, was different from Britain's in several key ways. While Parliament could only impeach the king's ministers, Congress could impeach the president of the United States, as well as the "Vice President and all civil Officers of the United States." (No, despite President Trump's claims, "officers" doesn't include senators like Mitt Romney.) And unlike in Britain, where Parliament could send an official to prison or to their death as a result of impeachment proceedings, in America, "cases of impeachment," the delegates wrote in the Constitution, would not "extend further than to removal from office."

As the convention wound down, the delegates had a solid idea of what impeachment would look like in the United States of America, but on August 31, 1787, the 98th day of the convention, there was one urgent question they still hadn't answered: what, exactly, would qualify as an impeachable offense?

In early drafts of the Constitution, the standard had been "malpractice or neglect of duty," but the delegates were worried that would leave Congress with too broad a mandate. So after months of procrastination, the delegates did what they always did when they could no longer afford to delay answering a difficult question: they assembled a committee. They called it the Committee on Postponed Matters. It consisted of one delegate from each of the 13 colonies, and it was tasked with determining what kinds of offenses would warrant impeachment.

Less than a week later, on September 4, the committee released a report determining that a president could be impeached only if found guilty of treason or bribery. But on September 8, George Mason lambasted this standard, arguing it would not "reach many great and dangerous offenses."

He was right: limiting impeachment to treason or bribery would be nowhere near as effective a check on the president's power as our founders intended it to be. The Constitution's definition of treason, after all, was deliberately very narrow, including only "levying war against [the United States], or . . . adhering to their Enemies." And the term "bribery," left undefined in the Constitution, likewise excluded a wide range of offenses the founders viewed to be impeachable, including the solicitation of foreign interference in an election. (For more on bribery, read Chapter 3.)

Mason's suggestion? Lowering the bar to include "treason, bribery, and *maladministration.*"

Madison, one of the members of the committee, agreed with Mason's rebuke of the treason-and-bribery standard but felt that including "maladministration" was an overcorrection. "So vague a term," Madison said, "will be equivalent to a tenure during pleasure of the Senate." Madison was afraid that this language would make the president more like a prime minister, subject to votes of no confidence by the legislature at any point.

Mason conceded Madison's point and sent back an edit that would change the course of American history. "Maladministration," he decided, would be replaced with "high crimes and misdemeanors against the state," a term borrowed from the English Parliament, whose meaning, as I'll explain on the following pages, has been debated ever since.

The committee voted 8–3 in favor of the new standard, changing it slightly to read "high crimes and misdemeanors against the United States." But the phrase's journey through the byzantine procedures of the Constitutional Convention was not finished. It still had to be approved by one more constituency: the Committee on Style.

This Committee on Style didn't have many responsibilities — and was explicitly barred from changing the substance of any statutes. Its sole purpose was to ensure that the Constitution would be written in a way that could be understood for centuries. So when its members received the language surrounding impeachment, they didn't plan to make any major revisions. And, in some ways, they didn't. They simply made the phrase "high crimes and misdemeanors against the United States" more concise, deleting the last four words.

The final text, which would come to comprise Article II, Section 4 of the Constitution, read as follows:

> *"The President, Vice President, and all civil Officers of the United States, shall be removed from Office on Impeachment for, and Conviction of, Treason, Bribery, or other high Crimes and Misdemeanors."*

This may seem like a minor edit, but in deleting four words, the Committee on Style played a role in bewildering generations of lawyers, politicians, and citizens who still debate what qualifies as an impeachable offense.

What High Crimes and Misdemeanors Are Not

This raises the question: What are high crimes and misdemeanors?

To understand what they are, it helps first to understand what they are not. That's because impeachment is designed to be rare, reserved only for a very specific kind of offense. And, in most cases, if you're wondering whether a president's actions are impeachable, the answer will likely be no.

Public opinion on what is and isn't impeachable is shaped by two widespread misunderstandings of the phrase "high crimes and misdemeanors." The first is that a president can be impeached *only* for crimes and misdemeanors laid out in the federal criminal code. The second is that a president can be impeached for *all* crimes and misdemeanors laid out in the criminal code. Both of these are wrong.

Let's start with the first. The idea that a president can be impeached *only* for violations of a criminal statute is atextual: the Constitution does not say that. Moreover, it is illogical, as it would exclude many abuses of power that our founders deemed clearly worthy of impeachment.

Let me offer an example. What if an incumbent president's opponent in the general election were murdered by the president's brother one day and the president pardoned his sibling the next day? According to the Constitution, the president's pardon power is unlimited "except in cases of impeachment," which means he would have the right to declare, based on the text of the Constitution, that what his brother did was, to quote President Trump, "very legal, very cool." And because this president controls the Justice Department, he could direct prosecutors not to charge his brother in the first place, before needing to use his pardon power.

But allowing a president to get away with this abuse of power would set a precedent that a sitting president could sanction the killing of his political opponents by supporters — a precedent that would make America more closely resemble a dictatorship than a democracy. So *of course* Congress could impeach the president for conduct like this, notwithstanding the language about pardons in Article II, and notwithstanding the fact that abuse of the pardon power isn't itself a criminal act.

This is an extreme case, but it's not an isolated one. There are many actions the president could take that are technically legal but would nonetheless warrant impeachment. In their book, *Impeachment: A Handbook*, law professors Charles Black and Philip Bobbitt provide a few illustrative examples. "What if," they write, "the president required all cabinet members to affirm their belief in the divinity of Christ? Or that he devolved to his personal financial adviser classified intelligence about upcoming decisions of the Federal Reserve? Because the president can declassify any material he wishes, there is nothing *per se* illegal about this."

Or, as they write, "What if the president announced that under no circumstances would he respond to the invocation of NATO's Article 5, which calls upon the signatories to the North Atlantic Treaty to defend each other when they are attacked?" What if we received evidence that our ally (say, France) was about to be attacked with a nuclear bomb by an adversary (say, Russia) and our president declined to tell leaders in Paris? What if we received evidence that *we* were about to be attacked by a nuclear bomb and our president declined to take action? Wouldn't that be cause for impeachment?

There's no law against the president keeping an impending nuclear strike secret from the American people — the commander in chief's wartime powers are nearly limitless — but of course this should qualify as an impeachable offense. Which is why we should never confine what may qualify as a "high crime and misdemeanor" to what's written down in our criminal codes. After all, the very first federal official to be removed from office through impeachment — a judge named John Pickering — was forced to step down in 1804 not because he violated any laws but because his drunkenness prevented him from ruling fairly on cases.

This brings us to the second misinterpretation of the phrase "high crimes and misdemeanors," which is equally mistaken: the idea that Congress can impeach the president for violating *any and all* criminal statutes.

If this were true, our democracy would exist in a perpetual state of chaos. We'd have presidents impeached for parking tickets, for jaywalking, for littering, and for all sorts of ridiculous offenses in the criminal code. In the important presidential caucus state of Iowa, for example, it's a misdemeanor to pass off margarine as butter — a deplorable thing to do, but certainly not a high crime or misdemeanor. If every criminal infraction were reason enough for impeachment, the results of our elections would last only as long as our presidents maintained perfect behavior. And our presidents would be forced to walk on eggshells every day for fear of breaking a law they don't even know exists.

We know this interpretation doesn't reflect the founders' views for many reasons — not least of which because they allowed Vice President Aaron Burr to get away with murder.

Literally.

If you've missed the *Hamilton* phenomenon of the last several years, here's the story: While serving in the second-highest office in the land, Vice President Burr killed Alexander Hamilton in a duel. And yet, Congress declined to impeach Burr, because they didn't believe his actions interfered with his ability to do his job. *Of course* he'd committed a crime. Murder always has been, and always will be, illegal. But in his case, they didn't believe it was a *high* crime.

Which raises the question: What does the word "high" mean in this context? Contrary to popular belief, the word "high" as used in the Constitution doesn't have anything to do with "the severity of the crime," as Jon Meacham, Timothy Naftali, Peter Baker, and Jeffrey Engel explain in their book, *Impeachment: An American History.* The term "high crimes," as the founders knew it, came from English law, where, to quote Meacham, it was defined as offenses "committed against the crown in a monarchy or the people in a democracy."

This is probably why the grammarians on the Committee on

Style deleted the phrase "against the United States," because they felt it was redundant with the word "high." Little did they know: "high" would take on many different meanings in the years ahead, and the debate over what exactly qualifies as a "high crime" would incessantly divide Congress over the course of American history, never more so than during the impeachment inquiries of President Andrew Johnson, President Bill Clinton, and President Richard Nixon, as well as the (abandoned) impeachment inquiry of President John Tyler.

THE IMPEACHMENT OF PRESIDENT JOHNSON

The moment Andrew Johnson swore his oath of office after Abraham Lincoln's death, one of America's greatest presidents was replaced with one of its worst. Where Lincoln was thoughtful, brilliant, and effective, Johnson was irascible, ignorant, and incompetent. While Lincoln spent his presidency uniting a house divided, Johnson spent his tearing America apart. Whereas Lincoln fought to end slavery, Johnson helped to ensure that its legacy would live on in America for centuries.

So there's no doubt our country would have been better off if Johnson had been removed from office. The problem was: he hadn't committed any impeachable offenses.

That didn't stop the House from impeaching him anyway. The "high crime and misdemeanor" they accused him of? Violating the Tenure of Office Act, a law Congress had passed only months before, barring presidents from firing any Senate-confirmed appointees without the consent of the Senate. The Supreme Court eventually ruled the Tenure Act unconstitutional, in 1926, but even back in 1868, as Johnson faced the prospect of impeachment, very few members of Congress earnestly believed he had committed an impeachable offense. They simply didn't believe he was fit to be president. And without another clear high crime to cite, they decided the Tenure of Office Act provided them with their best chance to remove him from office.

The crazy part was: It almost worked.

The House voted to impeach President Johnson by a margin of 126–47 — before he avoided conviction and removal by a single vote in the Senate, from a man by the name of Edmund Ross.

An abolitionist senator from Kansas, Ross didn't support President Johnson's policies. Far from it: Ross had aided antislavery militias before the Civil War. But he couldn't bear to impeach a president for anything less than treason, bribery, or another high crime or misdemeanor. So he voted against removing President Johnson from office, even though he knew he would lose reelection for doing so.

For nearly a century, Senator Ross's legacy was largely lost to the annals of history — until President John F. Kennedy included him in his book *Profiles in Courage*. Kennedy was no fan of Andrew Johnson, but he, like Senator Ross, believed our democracy depended on reserving impeachment for treason, bribery, high crimes, and misdemeanors. And while President Johnson's actions may technically have violated a statute, Kennedy knew they didn't meet the standards for an impeachable offense in our Constitution.

It's one thing to talk about living by the Yardstick Rule, another to actually do it, as Senator Ross did. That's why Kennedy believed Ross was a profile in courage. "In a lonely grave he lies, forgotten, unknown," Kennedy wrote of Ross. "He acted for his conscience and with a lofty patriotism, regardless of what he knew must be the ruinous consequences to himself. He acted right."

Ross's legacy looms over our discussion about impeachment

today, and serves as a reminder that even in the heat of the moment, we must not let short-term political expediency triumph over our long-term national principles. If we're going to impeach a president, in other words, it better be for an actual high crime or misdemeanor.

THE IMPEACHMENT OF PRESIDENT CLINTON

The story of President Clinton's impeachment follows a similar arc.

There is no denying that our 42nd president lied under oath. "I did not have sexual relations with that woman," he insisted, when he did in fact have sexual relations with his intern, Monica Lewinsky. President Clinton was guilty of perjury — and perjury is undoubtedly a crime. But was it a high crime?

The answer is: It depends (on what you're lying about).

Imagine President Clinton had lied under oath about a topic that directly impacted his ability to serve as commander in chief. For instance, suppose he had been spying on a political opponent's campaign but had sworn he hadn't done so. Or imagine he had lied about aiding an enemy of the United States in exchange for personal profit. In these cases, perjury would clearly qualify as a high crime, because the lies would obstruct investigations into underlying impeachable offenses.

President Clinton's lies about Monica Lewinsky were also reprehensible, and so was his conduct. He exploited perhaps the biggest power imbalance in the history of workplaces, between an intern and the president of the United States, for his own sexual gratification. He lied about it. And there's reason to believe this wasn't an isolated incident.

So why wasn't he convicted and removed? Because, as Laurence Tribe and Joshua Matz write, "While Clinton's conduct was faithless to his marriage and to the court in which he testified, it hardly broke faith with the nation as a whole or foreshadowed grave peril if he remained in office." Congress believed, in Tribe and Matz's words, that "ordinary checks and balances seemed fully capable of addressing any further objections to how Clinton conducted himself while in office."

So on February 12, 1999, Clinton was acquitted on all counts of impeachment — not only because the Senate didn't believe his actions rose to the level of a high crime, but also because of the nakedly partisan, and hypocritical, conduct of those impeaching him. Fundamentally, the American people did not believe President Clinton was being impeached in good faith. And, before long, they were proven right. As Jeffrey A. Engel writes, "Each of the three men who led House Republicans during Clinton's impeachment [Newt Gingrich, Bob Livingston, and Dennis Hastert] would ultimately face ridicule, ouster, and even [in one case] prison for their infidelities and sexual crimes."

Whether the Senate came to the right conclusion in declining to convict Clinton is for history to decide, but no matter what, his case teaches us two important lessons. The first is that perjury and obstruction, standing alone, are not sufficient reason to impeach a president — unless they're covering up underlying conduct that would qualify as a high crime or misdemeanor.

The second is that Congress needs to demonstrate that it is impeaching the president to protect the rule of law, not just to score political points. As soon as it becomes clear that an impeachment inquiry has been launched on the basis of what party the president belongs to or what he believes in — as soon as it's clear that legislators are using a different yardstick for a president of a different party than they would a president of their own — the case is over.

As it should be.

THE (BOTCHED) IMPEACHMENT OF PRESIDENT TYLER

This played out most explicitly during the presidency of John Tyler, which began in April 1841, after William Harrison died only 32 days into his presidency. Tyler was the first vice president in American history to ascend to the presidency without being directly elected to the highest office, so his tenure began on shaky ground — which, as Ronald Shafer argues, was made even shakier by the fact that Tyler's and Harrison's ideologies didn't neatly align. Whereas Harrison had long been a proud member of the Whig Party, Tyler had just recently relinquished his label as a member of the rival Democratic Party.

This worried Whigs in Congress — and their fears were confirmed when Tyler started regularly vetoing their bills. Before long he was kicked out of the Whig Party, and his closest friend in Congress, Henry Wise, was punched on the House floor by a Whig named Edward Stanly. "He lies like a dog," Stanly said of Tyler.

In July of 1842 these disagreements boiled over when Virginia representative John Minor Botts filed the first petition for impeachment in the history of the United States "on the grounds of [President Tyler's] ignorance of the interest and true policy of this Government."

"If the power of impeachment is not exercised by the House in less than six months," Botts threatened, "ten thousand bayonets will gleam on Pennsylvania Avenue."

But even many Whigs in Congress knew they couldn't impeach a president for purely political reasons. And ultimately, Tyler's opponents in Congress decided they had no choice but to wait until the next election — so they never even brought impeachment up for a floor vote. As Senator Henry Clay put it, "Let him serve out his time and go back to Virginia from whence the Whigs have bitter cause to lament that they ever sent him forth."

Our Constitution, Clay recognized, calls on members of Congress to vote to impeach the president only when the interests of their country, not their party, demand they do so, which is why, despite Botts's bluster, ten thousand bayonets didn't end up on Pennsylvania Avenue after all.

What High Crimes and Misdemeanors Are

Like most of American history, most of this chapter has been defined by what high crimes and misdemeanors aren't. They aren't *any and all* crimes, as President Johnson's case proves. They aren't *only* crimes as defined by our criminal codes, as Aaron Burr's unprosecuted murder proves. And they aren't cases grounded predominantly in political differences, as President Clinton's and President Tyler's cases prove.

Earlier in this chapter I broadly defined "high crimes and misdemeanors" as offenses committed against "the people," but I haven't explained what exactly that means or provided many specific examples. This is in part because so few elected officials have been impeached in our history, so while there's some precedent for what *doesn't* qualify as an impeachable offense, there's far less precedent for what *does*. But it's also because our Constitution does not provide a specific definition of the term "high crimes and misdemeanors." Our founders simply assumed we'd know what they meant.

As Rufus King, a delegate at the Constitutional Convention, was quoted as saying at the time: "It was the intention and honest desire of the Convention to use those expressions that were most easy to be understood and least equivocal in their meaning."

Needless to say, King failed at his job.

Since the convention, scholars, lawyers, and legislators have debated the meaning of the phrase "high crimes and misdemeanors." And we still do not have a specific definition written into our laws. But from notes taken during the Constitutional Convention and from the *Federalist Papers,* we do know what kind of president Congress was meant to remove — one who wielded the powers of the office for their personal benefit instead of for the benefit of the people.

This is why, as I indicated in the introduction, the best understanding of "high crimes and misdemeanors" is captured by Alexander Hamilton's description of an impeachable offense in *Federalist No. 65* as being an "abuse or violation of some public trust," relating "chiefly to injuries done immediately to the society itself." And we have one example from American history of a commander in chief who resigned for committing exactly that kind of offense.

THE IMPEACHMENT OF RICHARD NIXON

The midnight to 7 a.m. shift at the Watergate Office Building belonged to a security guard named Frank Wills, who was paid $80 a week for his services. Most nights he didn't have much to do. He'd walk around the building a few times, make sure no one had entered, and leave the next morning.

But late in the night on June 17, 1972, Frank saw something he hadn't seen before: tape holding doors open around the building. At first Frank assumed that the tape had been put up by the maintenance staff, so he removed it from the doors and went across the street to Howard Johnson's Motor Lodge to pick up food.

But when he returned, and found the doors had once again been taped open, he knew that what he'd seen wasn't normal. As he wrote in the security logs: "1:47 AM Found tape on doors; call police to make . . . another inspection."

This marked the beginning of Watergate, a scandal that would end the Nixon presidency, change the course of American history, and become the etymological precursor for a plethora of controversies both real and fake to follow, from Deflategate to Pizzagate.

But for more than two years after Frank Wills discovered tape on the doors of the Watergate building, President Nixon didn't step down from office. And for a long time, the country didn't even know that the Committee to Reelect the President — mockingly referred to as CREEP — had anything to do with the break-in.

But then, to use a cliché, the dam started to break.

On August 1, the *Washington Post* found a $25,000 check written by Nixon's campaign to one of the burglars, an early story in what would become one of the most legendary streaks of investigative journalism in American history, as reporters Bob Woodward and Carl Bernstein added revelation after revelation — about the burglars, the money they were paid, and the efforts of the White House to cover up the involvement of campaign officials.

In April of the next year, two of Nixon's closest aides, John Ehrlichman and H. R. Haldeman, stepped down. Soon, even Nixon had to acknowledge his campaign's involvement in the break-in, conceding in a prime-time address to the nation that he took "responsibility" for the "abuses that occurred."

Yet, in November 1973, 17 months after the break-in, Nixon still insisted that he was "not a crook." And Congress had difficulty proving him wrong, because Nixon did everything he could to minimize his cooperation with its impeachment inquiry. This included stonewalling Congress and asserting executive privilege to avoid turning over tapes that implicated him and his staff in criminal activity.

This didn't go well for him. In a unanimous ruling, signed by three justices appointed by none other than Nixon himself, the Supreme Court ordered Nixon to release the tapes. Executive privilege, they declared, "cannot prevail over the fundamental demands of due process of law." No one, not even the president, they explained, was above the law.

In response to the Court's ruling, members of Congress from Nixon's party visited him at the White House and demanded that he step down. Recognizing that he had no chance of escaping impeachment, and "abhorrent to every instinct in [his] body," he resigned in a matter of days.

Why was Nixon's fate so different from Johnson's and Clinton's? The answer isn't just that Nixon committed violations of federal law; in most readings of the law, so too did Johnson and Clinton. And it isn't just that he obstructed justice, a crime Clinton was almost certainly guilty of as well.

The reason Nixon was going to be impeached, if he had not resigned, was that the crime he was covering up — a burglary of his political opponent's headquarters — was an "abuse of public trust," in that it undermined our democracy itself. It was, in other words, a *high* crime, a crime against the people, one Democrats and Republicans would both see as fundamentally wrong and at odds with American democracy, as long as they applied the Yardstick Rule. And it was exactly that kind of offense — a public servant putting their interests above the nation's — that our founders wanted to prevent a president from ever committing.

After all, the framers viewed the president as a fiduciary, the government of the United States as a sacred trust, and the people of the United States as its beneficiaries. The central manner in which they feared a president would break his oath of office was if he engaged in self-dealing — if he profited personally from his position at the expense of the people he served.

President Nixon violated that oath as soon as he deployed his powers as president to cover up evidence of a crime committed to benefit himself, which is why I'm confident our founders would have believed he should have been impeached. But as much as they disdained ordinary electoral interference of the type Nixon covered up, there was one thing they feared even more: a president who pursued electoral interference from a foreign power.

Why Our Founders, and Past Presidents, Were So Afraid of Foreign Interference

As President Trump's phone call with President Zelensky started to raise questions, the *New York Times*'s Peter Baker called up 10 former White House chiefs of staff, who had worked under Obama, Bush Jr., Clinton, Bush Sr., and Reagan. He asked them whether they'd ever work with a foreign power to win an election. Every single one of the chiefs of staff provided Baker with a definitive no.

James A. Baker III, George H. W. Bush's chief of staff, recalled a day in October 1992 when President Bush was approached by four Republican members of Congress who had an idea for how he could win reelection. "They told him the only way to win was to hammer his challenger Bill Clinton's patriotism for protesting the Vietnam War while in London and visiting Moscow as a young man," Baker writes. Bush didn't reject the idea out of hand; in fact, he thought it might work. But when Baker heard that the only way to reveal this information would be to "contact the Russians or the British," he realized that the administration "absolutely could not do that."

Why would someone as canny and strategic as Baker be so opposed to the idea of asking a foreign power to help his boss win an election? Because opposition to foreign interference in our elections is as old as America itself.

At the beginning of this book, I mentioned Washington's belief that "foreign influence is one of the most baneful foes of republican government," Adams's fear that "the danger of foreign influence" would "recur" as "often as elections happen," and Madison's belief that we needed impeachment in our Constitution to ensure that no president would "betray his trust to foreign powers." These comments represent only a glimpse into the founders' fear of other nations invading our democracy. *Federalist No. 68*, written by Alexander Hamilton, warned that the "most deadly adversaries of republican government" would come "chiefly from the desire in foreign powers to gain an improper ascendant in our councils."

"How could they better gratify this," he added, "than by raising a creature of their own to the chief magistracy of the Union?"

This apprehension of foreign actors — shared by Hamilton, Washington, and Madison alike — affected our Constitution in multifarious ways. It led to the natural-born citizen clause, which states that "No Person except a natural born Citizen, or a Citizen of the United States, at the time of the Adoption of this Constitution, shall be eligible to the Office of President." It led to the emoluments clause, which states that "no Person holding any Office of Profit or Trust under them . . . shall . . . accept of any present, Emolument, Office, or Title, of any kind whatever, from any King, Prince, or foreign State." And, of course, it led to the Constitution granting Congress the power to impeach a president. The latter two of these constitutional provisions were linked together. As Edmund Randolph told the Virginia Ratifying Convention, a president "may be impeached" for "receiving emoluments from foreign powers."

Within years of the Constitution's ratification, the founders' worst fears were confirmed: foreign officials had begun to interfere in our democracy. As historian Jordan Taylor writes: "Throughout the 1790s, France's ambassadors repeatedly sought to influence the results of American elections, hoping to sway policy in their favor." When Edmond-Charles Genêt, France's ambassador to the United States, failed to influence President George Washington's foreign policy, Genêt threatened to launch a persuasion campaign on voters themselves. Washington, wary as ever of foreign influence, asked France to fire him — a request the French government fulfilled.

However, Genêt's successors, Jean Antoine Joseph Fauchet and Pierre-Auguste Adet, were no better. Indeed, both of them tried to sway the US elections in one way or another. But President Washington refused to let them hold any influence over our democracy — and neither did the American people. To quote Taylor:

"One newspaper writer exhorted Americans to 'be on your guard, this is the crisis, when foreign powers will make their great effort to secure a lasting influence over your affairs and Direct Your Government.' Another essayist, signing his name 'National Pride,' remarked, 'If the choice of a President of the United States is to depend on any Act of a foreign nation, farewell to your liberties and independence.'"

"These Americans understood," concludes Taylor, "that allowing a foreign adversary to determine the outcome of elections would mean the death of their experiment in democracy."

These are the stakes of President Trump's impeachment. Like President Nixon, he abused the public trust by wielding the powers of the presidency to serve himself instead of the public. But unlike President Nixon, he didn't do it solely with the assistance of fellow Americans; he did it by seeking help from a foreign power.

That makes President Trump's high crimes even worse. And if we fail to hold him accountable, as our founders feared, I believe that could very well mark the end of the American experiment.

2

THE EVIDENCE

After much study and reflection, I have come to the view that President Trump should be removed from office. That's no state secret. The title of this book kinda gives it away.

But I promise: This chapter is not informed by my opinions on President Trump's conduct. I will save those for later. My only goal here is to set out the facts, so you can decide for yourself whether or not President Trump should remain in the Oval Office.

Of course, new facts may very well have come to light since this book went to press, but the evidence described here, alone, is more than enough to impeach President Trump — and it can only get worse.

Here's what happened.

"If Foreign Powers Offer You Information on Your Opponents, Would You Accept It?"

Early in the summer of 2019, George Stephanopoulos of ABC asked President Trump a simple question: if foreign powers offer you information on your opponents, would you accept it? The president answered without missing a beat. "I think you might want to listen, there isn't anything wrong with listening," he said. "If somebody called from a country . . . [saying] 'we have information on your opponent,' I think I'd want to hear it."

When President Trump's comments aired, as *The New Yorker*'s John Cassidy noted at the time, even his allies had a hard time justifying them. "I'm not here to defend Trump's interview with Stephanopoulos," Fox News's Tucker Carlson said, before qualifying his statement: "Why would you give an interview to Stephanopoulos in the first place?" Sean Hannity resorted to bestowing upon Stephanopoulos a Trumpian nickname: "Little Georgie." Representative Tom Cole, a Republican from Oklahoma, went so far as to say that accepting assistance from a foreign power is "not an appropriate way to behave in a political campaign." Even Republican senator Lindsey Graham, a loyal Trump ally, said that "it should be practice for all public officials who are contacted by a foreign government with an offer of assistance . . . to inform the FBI and reject the offer."

A Trump Administration official, Ellen Weintraub, who runs the Federal Election Commission, actually condemned President Trump's statements in public. "Let me make something 100 percent clear to the American public or anyone running for public office," she said. "It is illegal to solicit, accept, or receive anything of value from a foreign national in connection with a US election."

As Cassidy wrote: "Even the late-night comics, who have been feeding on Trump's gaffes for years, were stunned." "The guy who has spent two years scream-tweeting 'no collusion!' is now saying, 'If anyone's down to collude, I'm your guy,'" Seth Meyers joked. "If Trump had been president during Watergate, he would have left a business card at the break-in," Stephen Colbert added.

Even President Trump, who is not known to express regret,

walked back his comments. "Of course you give it to the FBI or report it to the attorney general or somebody like that," he conceded on *Fox and Friends*. "You couldn't have that happen with our country — and everybody understands that, and I thought it was made clear."

As it turned out, President Trump was being honest the first time. Because a scant 43 days after his interview with Stephanopoulos, he didn't merely accept foreign interference. He asked for it.

In Chapter 3, I elaborate on why this request of President Trump's was an impeachable offense, but for now, I want to present you with the timeline of what took place. The facts alone, from 2014, when Russia annexed Crimea, to 2019, when President Trump asked for Ukraine to interfere in our elections (and then covered it up), demonstrate how our commander in chief took advantage of the powers of his office to improve his chances of winning the 2020 presidential election.

The Decision to Withhold Security Assistance from Ukraine (and the Plan for the Phone Call)

In 2014, Russia annexed a peninsula called Crimea from Ukraine — and Ukraine has been forced to contend with Russian aggression ever since. So as part of the 2016 National Defense Authorization Act, the United States started the Ukraine Security Assistance Initiative, ensuring Ukraine's military would have the training and equipment they need to fend off future attacks from Russia.

In June of 2019, as had become a yearly ritual, Congress announced it would be including security assistance for Ukraine in the 2020 National Defense Authorization Act. As Republican senator Rob Portman, who cofounded the Senate Ukraine Caucus, said upon approval of the funding, "This security assistance package is good news, and it sends a clear message that America stands with the Ukrainian people in their struggle to secure a democratic, prosperous, and independent future in the face of Russian aggression."

Together, the State Department and the Department of Defense were set to send Ukraine $391 million in military aid, but at the last minute, President Trump ignored the Office of Management and Budget's rules and ordered it withheld. At the time, President Trump didn't provide an explanation for his actions. The State Department and the Department of Defense were simply directed by the White House to communicate to members of Congress that there had been an "interagency delay."

Ambassador William Taylor, who was then the top US official in Ukraine, said that he didn't find out about the hold until it had already been implemented. "Toward the end of an otherwise normal [National Security Council video-conference] a voice on the call — the person was off-screen — said that she was from OMB and that her boss had instructed her not to approve any additional spending of security assistance for Ukraine until further notice," Ambassador Taylor recalled. "I and others sat in astonishment. The Ukrainians were fighting the Russians and counted on not only the training and weapons, but also the assurance of US support."

Why had the United States made this decision — let alone without the input of Ambassador Taylor? "All that the OMB staff person said was that the directive had come from the president to the Chief of Staff to OMB," Taylor remembered. "One of the key pillars of our strong support for Ukraine was threatened."

Soon thereafter, according to Ambassador Taylor's testimony to Congress, "the Defense Department was asked to perform an analysis of the effectiveness of the assistance. Within a day, the DOD came back with the determination that the assistance was effective and should be resumed."

And yet — the assistance still wasn't released.

For weeks, US officials kept this hold hidden from the public, but Ambassador Taylor came to understand that the only way the assistance would be released was if President Zelensky agreed to open up two investigations. The first would be into whether a company called CrowdStrike had falsely blamed Russia for hacking the Democratic National Committee in 2016. The second would be into Vice President Joe Biden's ties to a Ukrainian company called Burisma. In fact, Ambassador Taylor learned, President Trump wouldn't even agree to a meeting with President Zelensky until the Ukrainian leader announced these investigations — an announcement that was supposed to be aired not on Fox News, but on the more neutral CNN.

This account is corroborated by a text that Kurt Volker, President Trump's special representative for Ukraine, wrote to Gordon Sondland, the United States ambassador to the European Union, stipulating the terms for a meeting. "Most impt," Volker wrote, "is for Zelensky to say that he will help investigation."

At first President Zelensky balked at the request to open investigations at President Trump's behest. As Ambassador Taylor noted in a text to Sondland, "President Zelenskyy is sensitive about Ukraine being taken seriously, not merely as an instrument in Washington domestic, reelection politics." But after weeks of discussions with members of the US government, President Zelensky finally scheduled a phone call with President Trump.

The Call

The phone call took place on July 25, exactly one day after Special Counsel Robert Mueller testified before Congress.

The conversation began not with hostility but with flattery. President Trump congratulated Zelensky on winning his election. And Zelensky, in turn, said he was "trying to work hard because we want to drain the swamp here in our country," referencing Trump's campaign slogan.

But after a few civil exchanges between the two leaders, President Trump began laying the groundwork for his request — channeling the kind of language often used by members of the Mafia before requesting a favor. "The United States has been very, very good to Ukraine," he said. "We do a lot for Ukraine. We spend a lot of effort and a lot of time." As Congressman Adam Schiff argued, President Trump might as well have said, "That's a nice country you have. It'd be a shame if something happened to it."

Over the course of mere seconds, Trump transitioned from saying the United States "has been very, very good to Ukraine" to claiming Ukraine hadn't been "reciprocal" with its generosity. Zelensky, for his part, did not dispute Trump's account, saying that Trump's analysis was "absolutely right — not only 100 percent, but actually 1,000 percent."

And then, Zelensky brought up the question of military assistance. "I would also like to thank you for your great support in the area of defense," he said. "We are ready to continue to cooperate for the next steps; specifically, we are almost ready to buy more Javelins from the United States for defense purposes." (These shoulder-fired missile systems are seen as an effective way to defend against incursions of Russian tanks crossing the country's eastern border — and they could have been funded in part with the aid Congress had approved but Trump was now withholding.)

President Trump's response to this comment marked the first moment he acknowledged the personal arrangement he had been trying to broker between the United States and Ukraine — in other words, the first moment he tried to establish a quid pro quo exchange. Sure, he indicated, he'd sell them the Javelins, before qualifying his answer: *"I would like you to do us a favor though."*

This favor, it turned out, consisted of opening the two investigations mentioned above. First he mentioned CrowdStrike, a company at the center of a long-debunked conspiracy theory about the 2016 election. "The server, they say Ukraine has it," President Trump said on the call. "I would like to have the Attorney General call you or your people and I would like you to get to the bottom of it," he declared.

But he didn't stop there. After a quick digression about the Russia investigation ("As you saw yesterday, that whole nonsense ended with a very poor performance by a man named Robert Mueller"), President Trump noted there was one "other thing" he'd like President Zelensky to investigate. "There's a lot of talk about Biden's son," he said, referencing Hunter Biden's work with a Ukrainian company called Burisma. "A lot of people want to find out about that," he went on, "so whatever you can do with the attorney general would be great."

Trump's claim on the call was that Vice President Biden "went around bragging that he stopped the prosecution" of his son — by encouraging Ukraine to fire a prosecutor named Viktor Shokin. Hunter and Joe Biden's activities were far from perfect (as I explain in Chapter 4), but the reality is that Shokin simply had not been investigating Hunter Biden or Burisma at the time of his firing. And in 2016, Republicans and Democrats alike advocated for his removal. As Republican senator Ron Johnson said, "The whole world felt that Shokin wasn't doing a [good] enough job." Senator Portman expressed a similar view. Shokin was removed because he "wasn't doing nearly enough to root out corruption," the senator said, "not because he was doing too much."

Nevertheless, when Trump asked Zelensky to look into Vice President Biden, the Ukrainian leader didn't reject the request. In fact, he went so far as to assent to it, promising to "look into the situation, specifically to the company that you mentioned in this issue."

President Trump then confirmed that Attorney General William Barr would be involved in this investigation as well, promising that he'd "have Mr. Giuliani give you a call and . . . have Attorney General Barr call." Viktor Shokin, he pleaded to Zelensky, one more time, "was treated very badly and . . . was a very fair prosecutor."

In response, Zelensky thanked Trump for the advice before closing the call the same way he opened it — by pandering. "Actually last time I traveled to the United States, I stayed in New York near Central Park and I stayed at the Trump Tower," he said, before promising once more that he "will be very serious about the case and will work on the investigation."

This promise to launch an investigation didn't only fulfill President Trump's first proposed quid pro quo, about the Javelins. It also met the specifications for the Trump Administration's second goodie, one only a president could dangle — a White House visit. In response to Zelensky's pledge to "work on the investigation," Trump said, "Whenever you would like to come to the White House, feel free to call . . . Give us a date, and we'll work that out," he added. "I look forward to seeing you."

This second quid pro quo — trading an investigation for a White House visit — didn't come about spontaneously but had been arranged by Trump's envoys prior to the phone call. "Heard from White House," Volker said in a text to one of President Zelensky's advisers, written before the conversation took place. "Assuming President Z convinces Trump he will investigate . . . we will nail down his visit to Washington."

With President Trump convinced of President Zelensky's intentions to investigate CrowdStrike and Vice President Biden — and with Zelensky promised a White House visit — the phone call came to a close.

"I look forward to seeing you in Washington," Trump concluded.

Zelensky responded, "Thank you very much, Mr. President."

After a few more pleasantries the phone call ended, with a deal between the two presidents in place.

WHAT WASN'T SAID

As startling as the "transcript" itself is, what's also notable is what was not mentioned in the phone call. President Trump didn't spend even a single moment discussing US national interests or Ukraine's efforts to contain Russia. The entirety of the call focused on President Trump's past and present political opponents.

Why, then, did President Zelensky, who — as Ambassador Taylor explained — claimed not to want to involve himself in "Washington domestic, reelection politics," oblige President Trump's requests?

There is no rational explanation other than that President Zelensky believed he needed to do so to extract concessions from President Trump.

But while Zelensky did secure a meeting with Trump after the phone call, for weeks and weeks, the security assistance never came.

"I Think It's Crazy"

The day after the phone call, Volker and Sondland headed to Ukraine, where they met with President Zelensky. They were there to provide "advice to the Ukrainian leadership about how to 'navigate' the demands that the president had made."

But whatever actions Zelensky took in the following days were clearly insufficient — because the aid never arrived. This distressed Ambassador Taylor, who didn't understand why the president would hold Ukraine hostage over political favors. After all, Congress had already appropriated this aid to Ukraine, so as more time passed, members of Trump's administration knew his refusal to send the funds to Kiev would raise eyebrows in Congress and in the press. And as predicted, on August 28, *Politico* ran a story with the headline "Trump Holds Up Ukraine Military Aid Meant to Confront Russia."

Over the course of the next week, Ambassadors Taylor and Sondland debated how best to deal with this situation. "Are we now saying that security assistance and WH meeting are conditioned on investigations?" Taylor texted. "Call me," Sondland replied.

As the days passed by, President Zelensky's refusal to publicly open up a probe of Vice President Biden persisted — and so too did President Trump's hold on sending Ukraine its military assistance. In fact, according to Taylor's testimony, Ambassador Sondland explicitly told one of President Zelensky's closest aides, Andriy Yermak, "that the security assistance would not come until President Zelenskyy committed to pursuing the Burisma investigation." And President Trump's demands didn't stop there. A private promise from President Zelensky, he decided, wouldn't be enough, because President Trump wanted the Ukrainian president "in a public box."

"Everything," Taylor explained, "was dependent" on Ukraine's compliance with Trump's demand. This, according to Taylor, was an order from Trump himself: "Ambassador Sondland told me that President Trump had told him that he wants President Zelenskyy to state publicly that Ukraine will investigate Burisma and alleged Ukrainian interference in the 2016 US election."

More than two months after Trump first directed the State Department and the Department of Defense to withhold the funding, Ambassador Taylor declared he'd had enough. "As I said on the phone," he texted Sondland, "I think it's crazy to withhold security assistance for help with a political campaign."

When Taylor sent that message, he and Sondland had been exchanging messages every few minutes, but suddenly Sondland went silent for almost five hours. Over the course of that time, the *Wall Street Journal* has reported, Sondland spoke to President Trump, whose White House had recently heard about a complaint from a whistleblower about all this — a complaint that would later unravel the entire scheme.

Finally Sondland wrote to Taylor: "I believe you are incorrect about President Trump's intentions. The President has been crystal clear no quid pro quo's of any kind."

September 9, 2019, Text Messages Between Taylor and Sondland

[9/9/19, 12:31:06 AM] **Bill Taylor:** The message to the Ukrainians (and Russians) we send with the decision on security assistance is key.

With the hold, we have already shaken their faith in us. Thus my
nightmare scenario.

[9/9/19, 12:34:44 AM] **Bill Taylor:** Counting on you to be right about
this interview, Gordon.

[9/9/19, 12:37:16 AM] **Gordon Sondland:** Bill, I never said I was "right."
I said we are where we are and believe we have identified the best
pathway forward. Lets hope it works.

[9/9/19, 12:47:11 AM] **Bill Taylor:** As I said on the phone, I think it's
crazy to withhold security assistance for help with a political campaign.

[9/9/19, 5:19:35 AM] **Gordon Sondland:** Bill, I believe you are incorrect
about President Trump's intentions. The President has been crystal
clear no quid pro quo's of any kind. The President is trying to evaluate
whether Ukraine is truly going to adopt the transparency and reforms
that President Zelensky promised during his campaign I suggest we
stop the back and forth by text If you still have concerns I recommend
you give Lisa Kenna or S a call to discuss them directly. Thanks.

Sondland's text should be read with more than a few grains
of salt—because not only did he wait hours to respond, and
not only did he speak to President Trump in the interim, but it
is unclear how or why Sondland became involved in President
Trump's dealings with Ukraine in the first place. Before President
Trump's victory in 2016, Sondland had been a hotelier—and his
central qualification to be ambassador seemed to have been his
$1 million donation to the Trump Inaugural Committee. Besides,
the ambassador to the European Union doesn't typically have jurisdiction over Ukraine, because, well, Ukraine is not in the European Union.

Moreover, according to the testimonies of both Trump aide Fiona Hill and Ambassador Taylor, Ambassador Sondland had been a part of Trump's campaign to open up these investigations in the first place. And in a remarkable press conference, White House acting chief of staff Mick Mulvaney later confirmed that President Trump had in fact been withholding foreign aid until Ukraine agreed to investigate Democrats, claiming that quid pro quo arrangements like these happen "all the time with foreign policy."

Even before the Mulvaney admission, Sondland's text had been widely read as a last-minute gambit to hide the quid pro quo so many in the president's orbit knew to have taken place — in the way a drug dealer, realizing he's speaking to an undercover agent, might say, "I believe you misunderstood me. I meant 60 units of Coca-Cola."

No wonder national security adviser John Bolton, upon hearing about what had been taking place between Washington and Kiev, reportedly said, "I am not part of whatever drug deal Sondland and Mulvaney are cooking up."

Ultimately, despite Sondland's last-minute attempt to cover up the offense in his September 9 text exchange with Taylor, President Trump's fate had in some ways already been sealed. One month earlier, a whistleblower filed a complaint with the Department of Justice. And in a few weeks, it would reveal much of what Sondland, Trump, and the rest of the administration had been working so hard to hide. This whistleblower was about to become the modern-day equivalent of Watergate night watchman Frank Wills. Only this time, the watchman knew right away that he was unveiling a deep abuse of power — and an attempt to cover it up.

A Whistleblower Report, Suppressed

On August 12, 2019, the whistleblower filed an anonymous complaint with the inspector general of the intelligence community. The inspector general is kind of like an ombudsman for the various intelligence agencies, and this one, Michael Atkinson, was appointed by none other than Donald Trump. But after IG Atkinson read the report (which you can read for yourself in the appendix to this book), he declared it an "urgent concern" and requested that the acting director of national intelligence, Joseph Maguire, send it over to Congress, as federal law commands.

Yet weeks went by without either Maguire or Atkinson telling a single elected representative about the whistleblower's report, let alone granting Congress access to the complaint itself. In a letter IG Atkinson sent to the House Intelligence Committee on September 17, explaining the delay, he stated that he and Maguire were at an "impasse." And suddenly, it was unclear whether the public would ever learn anything about what was going on.

That's not what's supposed to happen.

Earlier in my life, I served as National Security Adviser at the Justice Department, where I got to see the extensive legal framework that governs our intelligence community in action. Before joining the government, I had watched too many spy movies about rogue agents, so I had no idea how regulated our intelligence services are. But once I understood the stakes of what they do, I immediately recognized why we needed clear guidelines for how to operate. Because, every day, human lives depended on us not messing up.

But I also recognized that such guidelines could be effective only if there were mechanisms for bringing wrongdoing to light. Because foreign policy and intelligence operations are by definition often secret, the system depends on women and men who come forward to report misconduct. And the only way they will come forward is if we have clear protocols in place to protect people like them. These are called whistleblower protections, and they are nearly as old as our nation itself.

Just seven months after the signing of the Declaration of Independence, the Continental Congress in 1778 passed a law proclaiming that "it is the duty of all persons in the service of the United States . . . to give the earliest information to Congress or other proper authority of any misconduct, frauds or misdemeanors committed by any officers or persons." In other words, our founders recognized that every citizen has a duty to report government wrongdoing — and should be celebrated, not punished, for doing so.

That law came about as a result of America's first whistleblowers, naval officers Samuel Shaw and Richard Marven, who in 1777 witnessed their commanding officer, Commodore Esek Hopkins, torturing British prisoners of war. There weren't any whistleblower protections in 1777, so Shaw and Marven lost their jobs as a result of their bravery — and indeed, their commanding officer went as far as to file a libel suit against them.

But the whistleblowers eventually complained to the Continental Congress that they had been "arrested for doing what they then believed and still believe was nothing but their duty." This prompted Congress not only to pass the aforementioned law protecting whistleblowers, but to relieve Hopkins of duty and compensate Shaw and Marven for what they'd been through, to the tune of $1,418.

Ever since, America hasn't only protected whistleblowers, we've relied on them to provide us with critical information, from Ernie Fitzgerald's alerts to Congress about the ballooning costs of the C-5 plane in the 1960s to Robert MacLean's revelation after 9/11 that the US government had been slashing the number of TSA air marshals on flights despite evidence that terrorists had been targeting planes. I know quite a bit about the latter, as I had the privilege of defending MacLean before the Supreme Court. When MacLean blew the whistle on a major terrorist threat that the government was trying to hide, he was rewarded with personal attacks before being fired. I took the case to defend what he did, and ultimately we won. The Supreme Court, in an opinion by Chief Justice Roberts, gave MacLean his life back.

The MacLean case is the last time the Supreme Court considered a dispute involving a national security whistleblower, and its decision had bipartisan backing. Indeed, in arguments to the Supreme Court in the MacLean case, a group in Congress led by Republican senator Chuck Grassley and Democratic senator Ron Wyden, as well as Republican representative Darrell Issa and the late Democratic representative Elijah Cummings, told the Supreme Court:

"Whistleblowers play a vital role in Congressional oversight of the federal bureaucracy. Members of Congress cannot station themselves or their staffs in agency offices to watch for evidence of malfeasance . . . Congress thus relies on individuals working within agencies to supply the information it needs to guard the public purse and give effect to the checks and balances that are essential to the separation of powers. By blowing the whistle, those individuals perform an invaluable public service."

One reason Congress appreciates the value of whistleblow-

ers is that our representatives have a unique window into the
necessity of their work. Whenever the inspector general of the
intelligence community receives a whistleblower complaint of
"urgent concern" that "appears credible," after the director of
national intelligence reviews the report, the law states that Congress "shall, within 7 calendar days," be forwarded "such trans-
mittal."

This process is critical — because protections for whistleblowers are meaningless if no one besides the inspector general and
the director of national intelligence ever finds out about their
complaints. But Acting DNI Maguire refused to follow through
on his obligation to send Congress the whistleblower complaint
within seven days and instead suppressed the report on President
Trump's conduct with Ukraine for weeks.

Thankfully, in the days after news of the complaint broke,
intrepid reporters nonetheless began to publish stories on what
information was conveyed in it. And soon, it became clear that
the complaint centered around a "promise" President Trump had
made to a foreign leader — but while rumors circulated that the
controversy had to do with Ukraine, nobody could confirm what
the promise was or to what country it had been made.

That is, until the night of September 19.

A Whistleblower Report, Revealed

That was when CNN host Chris Cuomo asked the president's
lawyer, former mayor of New York City Rudy Giuliani, if he had
requested the Ukrainian government to investigate Vice President Biden. "No, I actually didn't," Giuliani answered. But when

Cuomo pushed him, the lawyer provided him with exactly the opposite answer: "Of course I did."

Giuliani's interview sent shockwaves across the country, and soon it became clear that not only had Giuliani asked Ukraine to investigate Vice President Biden but so too had President Trump *himself* on a phone call with President Zelensky. With every hour, Congress made more requests for the Trump Administration to release the whistleblower's complaint. But the administration refused.

So on September 24, more than a month after the whistleblower filed their report but only five days after the pieces started to be put together publicly, the Senate unanimously passed a resolution calling for the release of the whistleblower's report. And House Speaker Nancy Pelosi decided that she would be opening an impeachment inquiry. "The actions taken to date by the president have seriously violated the Constitution," she said, declaring, "No one is above the law."

The following morning, with pressure mounting after Re-publicans and Democrats alike called on President Trump to send the whistleblower complaint to Congress, the Trump Ad-ministration released what it pawned off as a transcript of Pres-ident Trump's July 25 conversation with President Zelensky — a five-page document that appeared to have been edited by the White House but nonetheless confirmed that Trump had pres-sured Ukraine into investigating his major campaign rival, Vice President Biden. (In Chapter 4, I explain why the "transcript," which is actually a summary of the conversation, based on the notes of those who witnessed the phone call, might not tell the full story. The document is also reproduced in full in the appendix.)

As soon as Congress read the "transcript," they demanded access to the whistleblower's full report. And on September 26 they would finally have it.

"The Horse Has Left the Barn"

The morning IG Atkinson released the whistleblower's complaint to Congress began as the morning the whistleblower's complaint might be suppressed forever. In a letter to the House Intelligence Committee, Acting DNI Maguire announced that the whistleblower's report had been, in effect, downgraded from "urgent" by the Justice Department's Office of Legal Counsel — an office, it's worth noting, that falls under the jurisdiction of Attorney General Barr, who was a subject of the report. (Notably, this Legal Counsel opinion has come under severe attack; in an extraordinary move, five dozen sitting inspectors general throughout the federal government criticized it in the strongest of terms.)

This ruling from the DOJ meant that IG Atkinson and DNI Maguire no longer had an obligation under the law to share the complaint's contents with Congress. And for a minute it seemed as though the whistleblower report might never be released.

But later that morning, as DNI Maguire was set to testify before Congress, demands for the release of the report intensified. And eventually, presumably with the unanimous Senate vote ordering the Trump Administration to turn over the whistleblower's complaint in mind, the report was declassified. "The horse," Maguire said, after more than a month of being forced to sit on the report, "has left the barn."

And, it turned out, the contents of the whistleblower report not only confirmed the media's reporting, but revealed an extensive cover-up of President Trump's phone call with President Zelensky.

The Report

By the time the report was released, nearly every word of it had already been verified by authoritative sources — including by the White House's own "transcript," in which President Trump asked President Zelensky to launch an investigation of Vice President Biden. This, many believed, provided reason enough to remove President Trump from office. But the whistleblower's distillation of what had happened was startling nonetheless, because it described a series of events that were exactly the kind presaged by our founders when they decided to include impeachment in our Constitution.

"In the course of my official duties," the whistleblower wrote, "I have received information from multiple US Government officials that the President of the United States is using the power of his office to solicit interference from a foreign country in the 2020 US election. This interference includes, among other things, pressuring a foreign country to investigate one of the President's main domestic political rivals. The President's personal lawyer, Mr. Rudolph Giuliani, is a central figure in this effort. Attorney General Barr appears to be involved as well."

This discovery alone would have justified the inspector general's categorization of the report as "urgent," but the whistleblower also added a whole new layer to the story: the cover-up.

THE COVER-UP

When President Trump and President Zelensky's call had concluded, the whistleblower explained, White House officials were "deeply disturbed by what had transpired."

"They told me that there was already a 'discussion ongoing' with White House lawyers about how to treat the call because of the likelihood, in the officials' retelling, that they had witnessed the President abuse his office for personal gain."

These White House officials, it turned out, believed the best possible response to the phone call was to cover it up. "In the days following the phone call, I learned from multiple US officials that senior White House officials had intervened to 'lock down' all records of the phone call," the whistleblower wrote, "especially the official word-for-word transcript of the call that was produced — as is customary — by the White House Situation Room."

"White House officials told me that they were 'directed' by White House lawyers," the whistleblower continued, "to remove the electronic transcript from the computer system in which such transcripts are typically stored for coordination, finalization, and distribution to Cabinet-level officials."

As the whistleblower reported, after being deleted from the White House's server, "the transcript was loaded into a separate electronic system that is otherwise used to store and handle classified information of an especially sensitive nature."

I worked with some of the most sensitive intelligence information our government possesses in two different administrations. So I know firsthand that only the highest form of protected information, called code-word information, resides on these separate "air-gapped" servers. They are manifestly not the place to store transcripts of calls with foreign leaders, which are generally classified at a lower level because it's important for officials without top clearances to be able to access them.

That's why the decision to lock down records of this phone call was a blatant abuse of the system — because it blocked people who needed the information from obtaining it, and did so for no reason other than to protect President Trump. And it was especially egregious because there's no evidence that highly classified information *of any kind* was discussed on the phone call. That's why it was so easy for the White House to completely declassify the memo once they faced political pressure to do so. And it's why astute readers who look at the White House memo itself in the appendix will see that it was marked "Secret," a very low classification ranking. That means it should have been on a system that handles secret materials or even a system that could handle top-secret materials, but it simply didn't belong in a system specifically reserved for the most highly classified materials.

The only apparent reason President Trump's lawyers would have requested that the notes be removed from the computer system was to shield him from the consequences of his statements. As the whistleblower wrote, "One White House official described this act as an abuse of this electronic system because the call did not contain anything remotely sensitive from a national security perspective."

In his appendix, the whistleblower reported that, according to White House officials, this was "not the first time under this Administration that a Presidential transcript was placed into this codeword-level system solely for the purpose of protecting politically sensitive — rather than national security sensitive information." The whistleblower did not specify what other calls had been treated in this way, but members of the press later confirmed this account: Over the course of his presidency, Trump's White House has similarly suppressed transcripts of conversations with Saudi Arabia's crown prince, Mohammed bin Salman, and Russia's president, Vladimir Putin.

As of this writing, the contents of those discussions remain a mystery.

RUDY GIULIANI'S PRESSURE CAMPAIGN

The whistleblower's complaint didn't end with the description of President Trump's phone call — or with the details of his administration's cover-up. The report also made sure to discuss what the whistleblower referred to as "circumstances leading up to the July 25 Presidential phone call," which proved President Trump wasn't acting alone.

The story began, according to the whistleblower, in March 2019, when articles "appeared in an online publication called *The Hill*," in which a Ukrainian prosecutor named Yuriy Lutsenko made a series of false claims about Democrats in the United States. Ukrainian officials, Lutsenko claimed, had "interfered" in the 2016 presidential election in collaboration with the Democratic National Committee. Vice President Biden, he added, had intervened to halt an investigation into a company on whose board his son Hunter had sat. And Lutsenko said that US Ambassador Marie Yovanovitch, who had been critical of his poor record on fighting corruption, had a "do not prosecute" list to protect Democrats.

President Trump's own State Department officials, for their part, have said this is an "outright fabrication." But Lutsenko had a relationship with President Trump's personal lawyer Rudy Giuliani, whom he had already met with twice earlier in the year. "I went to his office and was there for several hours over three days," Lutsenko later told a reporter. Giuliani claimed he did this "at the request of the State Department" and has "all the text messages to prove it."

"When I talked to [Secretary of State Mike Pompeo]," Giuliani said on CBS, "he said he was aware of it." Secretary of Energy Rick Perry has confirmed that he'd been told that Giuliani had authority to lead on policy efforts related to Ukraine as well. Even Ambassador Sondland told Congress, "My understanding was the president directed Mr. Giuliani's participation, that Mr. Giuliani was expressing the concerns of the president."

So perhaps it's no surprise that, on April 25, 2019, President Trump went on Fox News to call Lutsenko's allegations "big" and "incredible." Because all evidence indicates that, having deployed Giuliani as his envoy, President Trump was at least in part responsible for the dissemination of these allegations in the first place.

Four days after that television appearance, Ambassador Yovanovitch, who had attempted to stop Giuliani from trying to influence Ukrainian policies through unofficial channels, was told to hop on "the next plane" back to Washington. And then, on May 6, she was let go, even though, according to her boss, she had "done nothing wrong."

"Although I understand that I served at the pleasure of the president," she told Congress, "I was nevertheless incredulous that the US government chose to remove an ambassador based, as best as I can tell, on unfounded and false claims by people with clearly questionable motives."

When Giuliani was asked in an interview to provide a reason for her dismissal, he said simply she was "removed because she was part of the efforts against the president."

About 72 hours after she was let go, on May 9, "*The New York Times* reported that Mr. Giuliani planned to travel to Ukraine to press the Ukrainian government to pursue investigations that would help the President in his 2020 reelection bid," wrote the whistleblower. "In his multitude of public statements leading up to and in the wake of the publication of this article, Mr. Giuliani confirmed that he was focused on encouraging Ukrainian authorities to pursue investigations into . . . alleged wrongdoing by the Biden family."

This might seem like a spectacular allegation from the whistleblower — but he didn't need any evidence to prove it. Giuliani himself had told the *New York Times* the reason for his visit to Ukraine, and he even went so far as to defend his conduct. "There's nothing illegal about it," he claimed in the article, before conceding: "Somebody could say it's improper." But with the spotlight on him, Giuliani decided to cancel the trip.

Around this time, according to the whistleblower, US officials became "deeply concerned by what they viewed as Mr. Giuliani's circumvention of national security decision-making processes to engage with Ukrainian officials and relay messages back and forth between Kyiv and the President." Ambassadors Volker and Sondland even spoke to Giuliani directly in an attempt to, as the whistleblower put it, "contain the damage . . . to national security."

These efforts, however, did not convince Giuliani to end his influence campaign in Ukraine. And "during this same timeframe," according to the whistleblower, "Ukrainian leadership was led to believe that a meeting or phone call between the President and President Zelensky would depend on whether Zelensky showed willingness to 'play ball' on the issues that had been publicly aired by Mr. Lutsenko and Mr. Giuliani." (By mid-May, I should note, Lutsenko had already retracted his claims about Joe and Hunter Biden.)

The phone call did not come immediately, but Giuliani refused to let up. "Shortly after President Zelensky's inauguration, it was publicly reported that Mr. Giuliani met with two other Ukrainian officials," both of whom "are allies of Mr. Lutsenko and made similar allegations," wrote the whistleblower. And after months of laying the groundwork, Giuliani finally organized a phone call between President Zelensky and President Trump. The rest, as they say, is history.

Though I should note that things have only gotten worse for Giuliani since the complaint was released.

As two of his aides were arrested for their work in Ukraine, Giuliani declined to respond to subpoenas in Congress, and reports indicate that he is under both counterintelligence and law enforcement investigations.

Regardless of what happens next with Rudy Giuliani — or with the investigation into President Trump writ large — the three events the whistleblower used to end their report tell you all you need to know about Giuliani's efforts to encourage Ukraine to interfere with the 2020 presidential election; and from whom he was taking orders.

The whistleblower wrote:

> "On 13 June, the President told ABC's George Stephanopoulos that he would accept damaging information on his political rivals from a foreign government."

> "On 21 June, Mr. Giuliani tweeted: 'New Pres of Ukraine still silent on investigation of Ukrainian interference in 2016 and alleged Biden bribery of Poroshenko. Time for leadership and investigate [*sic*] both if you want to purge how Ukraine was abused by Hillary and Clinton people.'"

"In mid-July, I learned of a sudden change of policy with respect to U.S. assistance for Ukraine."

President Trump's Shifting Defenses

As soon as the whistleblower's report was released, President Trump began fighting back against its accusations, but Trump and his allies had already been preemptively defending their actions.

"The reality is the president of the United States has every right to say to a leader of a foreign country, 'You got to straighten up before we give you a lot of money,'" Giuliani had said in an interview on September 22, days before the transcript was released. "It is perfectly appropriate," he continued, for Trump "to ask a foreign government to investigate this massive crime that was made by a former Vice President."

The following day, in a conversation with reporters at the United Nations, President Trump stayed on message. "If you don't talk about corruption, why would you give money to a country that you think is corrupt?" he said. "So it's very important that on occasion you speak to somebody about corruption."

The argument fell apart. At the Supreme Court, there's a moment in an oral argument when you can see an advocate's entire case collapse because they can't answer a devastating question without resorting to platitudes or nonsense. That's exactly what happened here. CNBC reporter Eamon Javers asked President Trump, "Have you asked foreign leaders for any corruption investigations that don't involve your political opponents?" Trump's answer: "You know, we would have to look, but I tell you — what I ask for, and what I always will ask for, is anything having to do with corruption with respect to our country." The dissembling was evident, just as in a bad Supreme Court argument.

Nobody, of course, would object to President Trump investigating corruption, but even members of his own party doubted the legitimacy of this argument. "When the only American citizen President Trump singles out," Republican senator Romney later tweeted, "is his political opponent in the midst of the Democratic nomination process, it strains credulity to suggest that it is anything other than politically motivated." This time it was a member of his own party saying that Trump had failed to follow the Yardstick Rule.

Making matters worse, Senator Romney's comments rang especially true, noted Samantha Vinograd, a former member of the National Security Council staff, because President Trump had recently *cut* the State Department's budget for fighting corruption around the world. "In the fiscal year 2019," she explained, "the bureau was granted $5 million, but State requested $3 million for fiscal year 2020 . . . If the president were really concerned about corruption in Ukraine," she concluded, "he and Secretary of State Mike Pompeo should have requested more resources."

The corruption argument also didn't pass muster because President Trump's administration had just written an official letter to Congress declaring "that the Government of Ukraine has taken substantial actions . . . for the purposes of decreasing corruption, increasing accountability, and sustaining improvements of combat capability enabled by US assistance." This letter, verifying Ukraine's efforts to combat corruption, is what provided Congress with a green light to send aid to Ukraine for yet another year in the first place. And it defies belief to assume that the Trump Administration did a 180 on its position regarding Ukrainian corruption in a few months, especially when Ambassador Taylor testified that there would have been no reason to do so.

The last reason the corruption defense doesn't work is that, according to Ambassador Taylor's testimony, President Trump asked President Zelensky to open up these investigations *publicly* (and on CNN specifically). If our president authentically cared about ending corruption in Ukraine, he would have had President Zelensky launch confidential investigations — interviewing sources, flipping witnesses, and trying to get to the truth — as law enforcement does day in and day out. I've worked on several law enforcement investigations, including some of the most sensitive ones. The one thing you don't do is publicly announce what you are doing. But President Trump didn't want a real investigation into the 2016 election and Vice President Biden. He wanted President Zelensky to make a statement *about* an investigation, which is simply not how you conduct a law enforcement operation. The demand for a public statement gave away the game.

Eventually President Trump realized that the corruption defense wouldn't be sufficient, so he offered up a new reason for why he had withheld the funding: Europe, he claimed, had not been contributing its fair share to aid in Ukraine. So, he asked, why would the United States carry its weight? "I'll continue to withhold [the funding]," Trump declared at the United Nations General Assembly, "until such time as Europe and other nations contribute to Ukraine, because they're not doing it."

Perhaps this argument would have distracted everyone for a bit if President Trump had not released the summary of his call with Zelensky the following day, which revealed that this wasn't about Europe's contributions to Ukraine's defense budget after all. For a few hours Trump simply ignored the backlash and insisted that the call had been "perfect." But when the whistleblower's report was declassified the next morning, Trump's allies wedded themselves to a yet another new defense: "hearsay."

As Senator Lindsey Graham tweeted, "In America you can't even get a parking ticket based on hearsay testimony. But you can impeach a president? I certainly hope not."

Two days later President Trump embraced this argument himself: "The so-called 'Whistleblower' has all second hand information," he tweeted. In audio from a private event published by the *Los Angeles Times,* President Trump went so far as to say he believed the whistleblower should be treated like a "spy." "He never saw the call," Trump exclaimed, before repeating it again: "He never saw the call."

"They're almost a spy," he continued, referring to the whistleblower. And he added that whoever had shared information with the whistleblower in the first place was "close to a spy" as well. "You know what we used to do in the old days when we were smart? Right? The spies and treason, we used to handle it a little differently than we do now," he concluded. The way "we" used to "handle" spies, of course, was by executing them.

The challenge with Trump's "hearsay" defense was that so much of the whistleblower's report already had been corroborated by authoritative sources. Indeed, the transcript of Trump's phone call with Zelensky didn't have a single discrepancy with the whistleblower's description of it. In fact, it showed Trump doing the very thing — asking a foreign power to investigate his political opponent — the whistleblower had alleged.

Whistleblowers, in my experience, sometimes get things wrong. They have only limited information and sometimes succumb to the all-too-human tendency to exaggerate. But this whistleblower was different: everything they said turned out to be verified by other sources, including, ultimately, by President Trump himself.

This isn't like receiving a parking ticket based on hearsay, as Senator Graham alleged. It's like receiving a speeding ticket based on a speedometer, a camera, and an admission from the driver that he was speeding.

Left without any evidence that the whistleblower's report had been fabricated—and with fear that another whistleblower, who did have firsthand accounts of Trump's actions, would come forward—Trump pivoted once again, adopting his most novel approach yet: defending his actions. "I have an absolute right," he tweeted, as I mentioned in the introduction, "to investigate, or have investigated, CORRUPTION, and that would include asking, or suggesting, other Countries to help us out."

Trump brought this message directly to the lawn of the White House, where he once again called on Ukraine to "investigate the Bidens" and, for good measure, shared his belief that "China should start an investigation into the Bidens" as well.

Acting chief of staff Mick Mulvaney distilled this message of President Trump's into a three-word phrase, "Get over it," which was later plastered on Trump campaign shirts.

President Trump has clearly come to believe that the best defense for his actions is doing them in public. *Why,* he hopes voters will ask, *would Trump be doing this in public if it were illegal?* This is the political equivalent of shoplifting a TV from a Best Buy and holding it above your head as you walk out of the store, hoping no one will question your behavior because you're acting so brazenly.

This Trump gambit—do it in public so no one cares—can be successful only for as long as our elected officials let it be. Forthrightness, once your crimes have been revealed, has nothing to do with whether you committed an impeachable offense. (Especially since President Trump's whole plan was to try to do this in secret—until he was caught red-handed.) If asking a foreign power to investigate a political opponent is a "high crime or misdemeanor," it shouldn't matter to Congress whether President Trump did it in public or in private.

That, perhaps, is why Trump pivoted once again and shifted to an even more grandiose tactic, one reminiscent of President Nixon's: refusing to cooperate with the House of Representatives' impeachment inquiry entirely.

When Speaker Pelosi opened that inquiry, President Trump declared that he wouldn't provide the House with documents its members requested. He tried to block a key witness, Ambassador Sondland, from testifying before Congress. Later that same day, President Trump's White House counsel, Pat Cipollone, sent a letter (which you can find in the appendix) to Speaker Pelosi announcing that President Trump would not participate in the probe. "In order to fulfill his duties to the American people, the Constitution, the executive branch and all future occupants of the office of the presidency," Cipollone wrote, "President Trump and his administration cannot participate in your partisan and unconstitutional inquiry under these circumstances."

Executive privilege, Cipollone's letter erroneously argued, provides the president with immunity from indictment, criminal charges, and even, in this case, impeachment. This resistance and obstruction is the very approach President Nixon took to his impeachment inquiry — an approach that led to his resignation.

Whether President Trump's fate will be the same remains to be seen. But this much is clear: President Trump believes he's above the law. And only Congress — with the American people behind it — has the power to prove him wrong.

In the next chapter, I'll tell you why we must.

3

THE CASE AGAINST
PRESIDENT TRUMP

If you've read the preceding chapters, you've seen that our founders believed we would be called to impeach a president who abused the public trust. And you've read about how President Trump has done exactly that. In this chapter, I connect the dots—explaining why President Trump's actions have left us with no choice but to remove him from office.

Whether or not you agree with my conclusion, I hope Americans from all parties will at least recognize that although the impeachment of President Trump may be conducted by politicians, it shouldn't be political. This isn't about what's best for Democrats or Republicans. It's about what's best for America.

Make no mistake: I believe the costs of removing President Trump from office are high. I worry doing so will further divide an already divided country. I fear President Trump's response to being impeached—and wonder whether he would rather stoke violence than accept Congress's decision. I feel for all the citizens who put their trust in President Trump and have been frustrated by those who have stymied his agenda. And I know our democracy might not recover from the removal of a duly elected president for a long time.

But as dangerous as President Trump's impeachment may very well be for our country, I believe it's nothing compared to the danger of letting a president like him off the hook.

Here's why:

The Pence Standard

The president of the United States has more power than any other human being on the planet — power our current commander in chief has deployed not to serve our country but to serve himself. In this way, he is precisely the kind of leader our Constitution's impeachment process was designed to remove, one who, to quote Vice President Pence, "put [his] own interests, [his] personal interests, ahead of public service."

That's the Pence Standard, and there's a reason it's one of the epigraphs of this book. Because Vice President Pence's distillation of what constitutes a high crime and misdemeanor is exactly in line with the founders' conception of the term. As Alexander Hamilton wrote in *Federalist No. 65,* impeachment was reserved for "those offenses which proceed from . . . the abuse or violation of some public trust . . . as they relate chiefly to injuries done immediately to the society itself." Like Vice President Pence, Hamilton believed Congress would be obligated to impeach the president only when he wielded the powers of his office for the benefit of himself instead of for the benefit of the people. That is the standard against which we will measure President Trump's conduct over the course of this chapter, one set by his own vice president. And, again and again, he will fail to meet it.

The Simple Case for Impeachment

There are so many strands to this story — so many interwoven tales filled with words like "interference" and "obstruction" — but the case against President Trump is simple.

He has:

> *Abused the public trust by soliciting foreign interference in the 2020 presidential election;*

> *Abused the public trust by engaging in bribery — repeatedly — through his quid pro quo exchanges with President Zelensky of Ukraine;*

> *Abused the public trust by obstructing justice into the investigations of his conduct, adopting an unconstitutional view of executive power;*

And worst of all:

> *He has promised to do it all again.*

Unless we stop him.

High Crime #1: Soliciting Foreign Interference

President Trump asked President Zelensky of Ukraine to investigate Vice President Joe Biden. This, alone, would be reason enough to impeach him.

Why? Well, let's be as generous as possible in our interpretation of what took place. Let's assume President Trump hadn't engaged in a quid pro quo ("something for something") exchange of any kind with President Zelensky, even though he did. Let's further assume he had lifted his hold on military aid to Ukraine *before the call* and had agreed to a White House meeting with President Zelensky *in advance,* even though in reality he didn't do either of those things. And let's assume Ukraine said no to the request to open up an investigation into Vice President Biden, even though President Zelensky did just the opposite on his phone call with President Trump.

President Trump would still have asked for help from a foreign power. And even if Trump's plan completely failed and Ukraine never did a thing, the offense of *solicitation* would have been committed.

That's because, in the law, solicitation is what is called an in-choate crime, which means the offer itself is the criminal act, regardless of whether or not it is accepted. And solicitation encompasses everything from offering to pay someone for prostitution to asking someone to commit murder.

Solicitation is a common criminal act, but President Trump's offense is a particularly dangerous form of it because he did everything he could to ensure that the American people would never find out about it — which, while good for him personally, meant that he opened himself up to blackmail. That is more than a crime. It's a massive abuse of the public trust—and therefore a clear impeachable offense.

Think about the leverage he gave Ukraine. "If you don't double our aid, or triple it, or quadruple it," Zelensky could have said, "then I'll tell the American people you sought to obtain foreign assistance in your election. And I'll look good, because I declined to give it to you."

Indeed, if the whistleblower had not revealed Trump's scheme, President Zelensky could have asked him for any favor under the sun and expected him to deliver on it, even if President Trump needed to undermine the interests of the United States to do it. That's why, regardless of whether Ukraine accepted Trump's request, his actions would still have warranted impeachment — because he would have jeopardized our national security either way.

If this fear of blackmail sounds familiar to you, that's because it isn't the first time this has happened under the Trump Administration. As you may recall, President Trump's first national security adviser, Michael Flynn, was successfully prosecuted for lying to the FBI. The reason this particular lie was so dangerous was that Russia knew it wasn't true, which meant they had substantial leverage over him. As Sally Yates, then the acting attorney general, put it, "This was a problem because not only do we believe that the Russians knew [he was lying], but that they likely had proof of this information — and that created a compromise situation, where the national security adviser essentially could be blackmailed by the Russians."

That is why it's such a damaging abuse of public trust for a government official at any level to involve a foreign power in a scheme they would like to be kept secret from the American people — because in doing so, they can be manipulated into serving the interests of that foreign power instead of the interests of the American people.

This time it wasn't the national security adviser who was at risk of being blackmailed but the president of the United States himself. The fact that President Trump was willing to put himself in that kind of compromised position — for the purpose of eliminating Vice President Biden from the presidential race — demonstrates that he is unfit to be president of the United States. After all, this is the primary evil our founders (and then-Representative Pence) warned against: a president who would use his power to benefit himself instead of the people he represents.

With President Trump, we've learned, it's not "ask what you can do for your country," it's "ask what a foreign country can do for you."

WHAT WE SHOULD (AND SHOULDN'T) CARE ABOUT WITH RESPECT TO RUSSIAN INTERFERENCE

As far as impeachment goes, I do not care whether or not President Trump "colluded" with Russia in 2016. Special Counsel Mueller said he did not have enough evidence to prove it, and I am inclined to believe him.

But here is what's undoubtedly true: President Trump and his campaign tried, over and over again, to collude with Russia. This may not in itself be an impeachable offense, since Trump wasn't president at the time and thus couldn't abuse his power, *per se*. It is nonetheless important context for what took place with Ukraine, because it's more proof that he is open to help from foreign powers.

As I alluded to in the introduction, at a news conference on July 27, 2016, Trump addressed Russia directly: "Russia, if you're listening," he said, "I hope you're able to find the 30,000 emails that are missing. I think you will probably be rewarded mightily by our press."

That same day, Russia began spearfishing attacks on 76 Hillary Clinton staffers. And before long John Podesta, the chairman of Clinton's campaign, clicked on the wrong link, providing Russia with access to thousands of his emails — which would later be posted by WikiLeaks just a few hours after a video came out in which President Trump said he likes to "grab [women] by the pussy."

The timing of Russia's attack and the release of WikiLeaks' emails may well have been a remarkable coincidence, but Trump's willingness to ask for foreign assistance was unambiguous. And over the course of the 2016 campaign, members of Trump's staff repeatedly followed suit, trying desperately to coordinate with Russia. In all, Mueller's report delineated at least 140 points of contact between Russians, WikiLeaks, and President Trump's associates. These included a meeting at Trump Tower between President Trump's son Don Jr., his son-in-law, Jared Kushner, his campaign manager, Paul Manafort, and a Russian lawyer named Natalia Veselnitskaya, who had ties to the Russian government.

Regardless of what information was communicated at the Trump Tower meeting, Trump's campaign had been told in advance that the discussion would focus on "very high level and sensitive information" meant to "incriminate Hillary." And, they were told, the meeting was only one element of "Russia and its government's support for Mr. Trump."

What, then, did Donald Trump, Jr., do when he was told that the Russian government would provide the campaign with dirt on Clinton? Did he do what any right-thinking person would do and write, "Um, thank you, can I get back to you?" and then pick up the phone to call the FBI? No. Instead, he wrote, "If it's what you say I love it especially later in the summer."

This meeting is the exact hypothetical Stephanopoulos asked Trump about: if a foreign power came to you with information on your political opponent, would you take it? The answer of Trump's 2016 campaign, it turns out, was the same one he gave to Stephanopoulos: "Yes." That's damning whether or not the campaign ended up succeeding in its efforts to collude with Russia. Because it showed President Trump wasn't only willing to cheat to win an election; he was willing to ask a foreign power to help him do it.

What's worse: as president, Trump has declined to hold Russia accountable for what Special Counsel Mueller described as "multiple, systematic efforts to interfere in our election." Russia's interference in 2016, the Mueller report revealed, wasn't limited to hacking John Podesta's email account. The Russians also launched disinformation campaigns on social media, sowed divisions in American political discourse, and went as far as to pay Trump supporters to wear costumes of Hillary Clinton in a prison uniform at rallies. They even penetrated the electronic voting systems of many states. This was a coordinated attack on our democracy, which President Trump has refused to do anything about.

In fact, according to the *Washington Post,* at a 2017 meeting in the Oval Office with Russian foreign minister Sergei Lavrov and Russian ambassador Sergey Kislyak, Trump communicated that he was "unconcerned" about Russia's interference in 2016. A former senior official in Trump's administration, quoted in the story, said Trump "was always defensive of Russia." He added, "He thought the whole interference thing was ridiculous."

Trump's failure to even acknowledge intelligence community reports proving Russia's interference — and his unwillingness to hold Russia accountable — were early signs that he didn't view foreign interference in our elections as an urgent threat. Indeed, we would later learn, he viewed it as an opportunity. That's the explanation for his answer to George Stephanopoulos, saying he would listen to "opposition research" from a foreign power. It's the explanation for the requests he made to President Zelensky over the phone. And it's the explanation for why President Trump asked China to investigate Vice President Biden, even after the House had already begun its impeachment inquiry into his dealings with Ukraine.

Fundamentally, President Trump doesn't have a problem with foreign interference in our elections — indeed, he encourages it — and he simply doesn't believe he will be held accountable for doing so. This is not only a high crime. It's the very one our founders feared most. And if we allow an incumbent president to get away with using the mighty constitutional powers of his office to pressure a foreign power into helping him win, our democracy might never recover.

High Crime #2: Bribery

But, of course, even though High Crime #1 is sufficient reason for impeachment, President Trump did, in fact, also offer quid pro quo exchanges to Ukraine. That's a form of bribery, one of the two impeachable acts that our Constitution specifically delineates as a "high crime and misdemeanor" in Article II, Section 4.

Now, the Constitution doesn't provide a definition of "bribery," nor, as Laurence Tribe and Joshua Matz note, "did federal law do so until 1853." So when evaluating President Trump's conduct, instead of asking exactly what the founders meant by "bribery," as Tribe and Matz argue, we are better off thinking about why "the Constitution singled out this offense."

As Gouverneur Morris, one of the early opponents of impeachment at the Constitutional Convention who later came around to being a supporter, explained, if bribery weren't an impeachable offense, a president "may be bribed by a greater interest to betray his trust." He feared, in other words, that without protections against bribery, the president could be persuaded to put his own interests above those of the people he serves.

Morris continued, in terms that are striking today, "No one would say that we ought to expose ourselves to the danger of seeing the first Magistrate in foreign pay."

For this reason, Tribe and Matz argue, our founders "built a multilayer defense system" against bribery, encompassing Article I's ban on emoluments (things of value given by foreign governments or states to the president) and the specific prohibition in the impeachment clause against bribery. "By writing bribery into the Impeachment Clause, they ensured that the nation could expel a leader who would sell out its interests to advance his own," Tribe and Matz write. This isn't only true when the president is the recipient of bribes, they continue. "It's also true when the president *offers* bribes to other officials."

"In either case," they conclude, "the president is fully complicit in a grave degradation of power, and he can never again be trusted to act as a faithful public servant."

But without a clear definition of "bribery" in our Constitution — and given that "bribery" wasn't even in the criminal code when our founders wrote the Constitution — how did they expect Congress to define it?

Well, our founders were common-law lawyers, focused not on legal technicalities but on the commonsense definition of bribery used by courts day in and day out. And that definition was pretty simple. As far as the founders were concerned, bribery occurred when a public official used his public powers for a personal benefit. In this sense, bribery is a clear violation of the Pence Standard.

William Hawkins's "A Treatise of the Pleas of the Crown" defined bribery this way in 1716: "Bribery in a large sense is sometimes taken for the receiving or offering of any undue reward, by or to any person whatsoever, whose ordinary profession or business relates to the administration of publick justice."

Notably, federal criminal law has moved in that direction, too (though remember my earlier caution that violating a specific statute is not at all necessary for impeachment). In the weeks after news broke about the president's call with the leader of Ukraine, many commentators focused on Section 201(b)(1), a provision in the federal bribery statute that says it is a crime to give or offer to a "public official" anything of value in exchange for performing an official act. Indeed, the mayor of Detroit, Kwame Fitzpatrick, was jailed for doing exactly this: demanding that his friend be cut in on various government contracts. But the term "public official" in Section 201(b)(1) is defined explicitly as a US official, not a foreign one, which means it's not exactly analogous.

So what does the law say about a US official soliciting a bribe from a foreign actor? A lot, actually. A separate provision in the law, Section 201(b)(2), says it is a crime if a public official (here, Trump) "directly or indirectly, corruptly demands, seeks, receives, accepts, or agrees to receive or accept anything of value personally or for any other person or entity, in return for . . . an official act." That fits Trump to a T. It is also a textbook definition of quid pro quo.

This is why quid pro quos are a big deal: because they are a form of bribery, which is an impeachable offense under the Constitution. And despite the protestations of Trump and his allies, the call between President Trump and President Zelensky featured not only one but two explicit demands of this kind.

The first came when President Zelensky mentioned wanting to purchase Javelins from the United States, prompting President Trump to say, "I would like you to do us a favor though."

This is about as blatant a quid pro quo offer as you will

find. That's why House leader Kevin McCarthy, one of Trump's staunchest defenders, denied that President Trump had ever said this during an interview with *60 Minutes*. "You just added another word," Leader McCarthy said, upon hearing the quote from CBS's Scott Pelley. "No, it's in the transcript," Pelley responded.

"He said — 'I'd like you to do a favor *though*'?" McCarthy asked, incredulous. "Yes," Pelley responded once more, "it's in the White House transcript."

Ross Spano, another Trump ally, made a similarly dubious argument to McCarthy in a speech on the floor of the House. "There is no quid pro quo," he said. "No this for that."

I've been a lawyer for a quarter century, so I can tell you: nobody literally says "this for that," but "I would like you to do us a favor though," is about as close as it gets. Even drug dealers know to take better care with their texts.

The second quid pro quo between President Trump and President Zelensky was the exchange of an investigation into President Biden for a visit to the White House. As discussed in Chapter 2, according to Ambassador Taylor, President Trump made clear before the call that he wouldn't agree to a meeting with President Zelensky until the Ukrainian said he would help with these investigations. And in a text exchange with a Ukrainian aide, Ambassador Volker made these terms explicit. "Heard from the White House," he wrote. "Assuming President Z convinces Trump he will investigate . . . we will nail down date for his visit to Washington." Quid, meet quo.

On the call itself, in direct response to Zelensky's pledging to "work on the investigation," Trump said, "Whenever you would like to come to the White House, feel free to call." That is, once again, about as cut-and-dried a quid pro quo as you will find. So over the course of a 30-minute phone call, Trump partook in two explicit quid pro quo exchanges, as defined by bribery law.

But as I've said, Congress doesn't even need to look at criminal codes to make the case that President Trump engaged in bribery, since even subtle offers of a quid pro quo from a president are grounds for impeachment. Why? Because whenever the president asks for a favor from a foreign country — with the power of the US treasury and the US military at his disposal — a quid pro quo is always implicit. After all, other countries know that a failure to do what the president of the United States asks could result in any number of negative repercussions, while a willingness to accede to his demands could result in any number of benefits. Even if it's not explicitly stated, that's all of the quid a foreign country needs to justify giving up a quo.

Now, I should note that this kind of implicit quid pro quo request is 100 percent acceptable when the president is asking for a favor *on behalf of the people*. If, for instance, President Trump asked England to share intelligence on a terrorist organization with the CIA in exchange for the US sharing intelligence about future threats to England, that would of course be aboveboard, as he would be eliciting intelligence *to protect the American people*.

The problem arises when the president asks a foreign power for a personal favor — one that doesn't align with the interests of those he represents. Because, as I mentioned in my discussion of High Crime #1, when a president abdicates his duty in front of another country, he leaves himself, and our nation, vulnerable to blackmail.

That's the abuse of trust. It's why our founders believed we needed to remove any president from office who would, in Madison's words, "betray his trust to foreign powers." And it's why they would be especially concerned by a president who has solicited bribes asking foreign officials to interfere in our elections over and over again — and shows no signs of stopping anytime soon.

High Crime #3: Obstruction of Justice

Compared to the severity of the core offenses President Trump has committed, Obstruction of Justice may seem like a petty crime. This is especially true because President Trump appears to be, well, pretty bad at obstructing justice. Not only have we learned about the high crimes he's committed in private, but we've also witnessed him asking foreign powers to help him win reelection in public.

And yet — as he has stonewalled Congress, refused to cooperate in the impeachment inquiry against him, and intimidated witnesses — President Trump has done more to obstruct the investigations into his conduct than any president since Richard Nixon, who ultimately resigned from office not because he broke into the Watergate building himself but because he obstructed the investigation into who did.

PRESIDENT NIXON'S OBSTRUCTION OF JUSTICE

In his conduct of the office of President of the United States, Richard M. Nixon, in violation of his constitutional oath faithfully to execute the office of President of the United States and, to the best of his ability, preserve, protect, and defend the Constitution of the United States, and in violation of his constitutional duty to take care that the laws be faithfully executed, has prevented, obstructed, and impeded the administration of justice.

So begins Article I in the impeachment of President Nixon, which details how Nixon wielded the powers of his office to obfuscate the truth about what happened at the Watergate building on the night of June 17, 1972. The charges leveled against President Nixon ranged from "withholding relevant and material evidence or information from lawfully authorized investigative officers and employees of the United States" to "interfering or endeavoring to interfere with the conduct of investigations by the Department of Justice of the United States." In all, Article I listed nine counts of obstruction — and based on these counts, as well as Article II, which focused on abuses of power, and Article III, which focused on disobeying subpoenas, the House Judiciary Committee voted to impeach him.

The charges themselves are dense — written in legalistic language — but they tell a story not dissimilar to the one we're living through today, in which a president's actions are driven not by a desire to serve the public but by a desire to hide the truth.

THE ACCIDENTAL WHISTLEBLOWER

Alexander Butterfield didn't have anything to do with the Watergate break-in. As deputy chief of staff, his role in the White House involved day-to-day tasks like handling President Nixon's schedule. So "when the Senate Select Committee on Presidential Campaign Activities published a list of people it intended to interrogate, Butterfield wasn't on it," as Alicia Shepard, author of *Woodward and Bernstein: Life in the Shadow of Watergate*, wrote.

"I was sort of surprised," Butterfield explained, "but relieved since I had nothing to do with Watergate."

Technically, this is true: Butterfield had nothing to do with the break-in at Watergate — or with the cover-up. But, in the end, he played as significant a role in the impeachment of President Nixon as just about anyone else.

When he was finally asked if he would speak to Senate investigators, on July 13, 1973, Butterfield, a lifelong Republican, had no desire to reveal any secrets about President Nixon. "If the investigators asked me an indirect or fuzzy question," he recalled, "I was justified in giving an indirect, fuzzy answer."

But when Butterfield was asked by one of the investigators, a Republican named Donald Sanders, whether there were any recording devices in the White House, he knew he had no choice but to answer honestly.

"Yes," Butterfield conceded — and thus, "The Nixon Tapes" were born.

Alexander Butterfield was no willing whistleblower. "Frankly, I don't like being known as the man who revealed the existence of the tapes," he said later. But his testimony in 1973 served the same purpose as the whistleblower's complaint did in 2019: revealing where to look for the crime.

Just as President Trump locked down the word-for-word transcript of his call with President Zelensky — which was mentioned by the whistleblower but has not been released — President Nixon did the same with his tapes, even after Butterfield's testimony. When Archibald Cox, the special prosecutor responsible for the investigation of the Watergate matter, issued a subpoena for the tapes, Nixon refused to comply. And even after the DC Circuit Court of Appeals sided with Cox, Nixon did everything in his power to limit access to the tapes.

As reporters Bob Woodward and Carl Bernstein wrote in their book, *The Final Days*, Nixon's allies had a creative plan by which they would keep the contents of the tapes from the public: "The President would personally listen to the subpoenaed recordings and supervise the preparation of transcripts that would be turned over to the court as a substitute for the tapes. The Prosecutor, long a bone in Nixon's throat and a bad idea in the first place, would be fired. That would eliminate the question of any litigation for still more of the President's tapes."

The president's advisers ultimately deemed this plan too dangerous, so they suggested a compromise: "Senator John C. Stennis, the seventy-two-year-old Mississippi Democrat who chaired the Senate Armed Services Committee, would be asked to make a comparison between the transcript and the tapes," wrote Woodward and Bernstein. The problem was that Senator Stennis was partially deaf, and, to quote Woodward and Bernstein, "the tapes were difficult to hear under the best of circumstances."

When Cox (understandably) declined to accept this deal on October 20, 1973, President Nixon ordered him fired — an event that would come to be known as the "Saturday Night Massacre," after Nixon also fired not one but two attorneys general who refused to carry out his directive. President Nixon hoped that removing Cox, as well as the attorneys general, would insulate him from the investigation, but when the Supreme Court ruled that he had to release the tapes, he was forced to accept that it would not.

The "smoking gun" tape, in and of itself, didn't do much more than confirm that President Nixon had been aware of the Watergate break-in — and had tried to impede the investigation into it. But once investigators understood its contents, they were able to weave together the story of a cover-up spanning multiple years, which, as Article I of Nixon's impeachment indicates, included everything from "making or causing to be made false or misleading public statements for the purpose of deceiving the people of the United States" to "endeavouring to cause prospective defendants, and individuals duly tried and convicted, to expect favored treatment and consideration in return for their silence or false testimony."

In Article III, Congress noted that Nixon also "failed without lawful cause or excuse to produce papers and things as directed by duly authorized subpoenas," which is an impeachable offense in itself. To quote Senator Lindsey Graham, who at the time of this statement was a member of the US House seeking to impeach and remove President Clinton: "The day Richard Nixon failed to answer that subpoena is the day he was subject to impeachment because he took the power of Congress over the impeachment process away from Congress and became the judge and jury."

Indeed, when all the evidence of Nixon's obstruction was put together, he was left with no choice but to resign.

PRESIDENT TRUMP'S OBSTRUCTION OF JUSTICE

The summary of President Trump's phone call with President Zelensky is to the Ukraine scandal what the Nixon Tapes were to Watergate.

Just as Nixon's administration did everything it could to keep the tapes under wraps, Trump's administration made a concerted effort to hide the transcript of his conversation with President Zelensky. As I mentioned in Chapter 2, the whistleblower detailed an operation led by White House lawyers to "'lock down' all records of the phone call," which prompted White House officials to remove "the electronic transcript from the computer system in which such transcripts are typically stored for coordination, finalization, and distribution to Cabinet-level officials."

This abuse of power — hiding a transcript of potentially criminal conduct — was only the beginning of President Trump's campaign to hide the truth.

Once members of his administration heard about the whistleblower's complaint, they did everything they could to prevent that report from reaching the public as well. As I mentioned in Chapter 2, complaints like these, labeled "urgent" by the inspector general, are supposed to be released to Congress on a pro forma basis by the director of national intelligence, since the laws governing whistleblower complaints say the DNI "shall" do so. But for reasons that are still unclear, DNI Maguire, along with the Department of Justice, denied Congress access to it.

The stated reason for doing so — which was that DNI Maguire worried releasing the complaint would risk violating executive privilege — didn't make sense on its face. After all, every whistleblower complaint involving the president by definition contains executive-branch-sensitive materials, so if DNI Maguire's analysis held, the president of the United States really would be above the law. That's why, eventually, just as Nixon was ordered to release his tapes, DNI Maguire felt compelled to send the whistleblower's report to Congress.

But before he did, the Justice Department joined DNI Maguire in trying to bury the whistleblower's report. In the face of a criminal referral from the general counsel of the CIA, the DOJ secretly concluded that President Zelensky opening an investigation into Vice President Biden wouldn't constitute a "thing of value" for Trump's campaign — and thus, deemed President Trump's request legal.

This decision didn't make any sense either, since the Justice Department had repeatedly stated in the past that "things of value" didn't have to be monetary and could include everything from a favor to a sexual relationship. Moreover, a longstanding memorandum of understanding between the DOJ and the Federal Election Commission required the FEC to be told of cases like this, because even if the DOJ declined to bring criminal charges, the FEC would retain the right to bring civil ones.

In this case, knowing an FEC investigation could become public, the DOJ blew off this policy, which had been in place for 40 years, and kept the matter hidden even from the FEC. This was especially surprising because, just six years ago, the FEC's vice chairman confirmed the existence of this very policy in a public memorandum he wrote.

His name?

Don McGahn — the same Don McGahn who would later become President Trump's White House counsel.

IS THE "TRANSCRIPT" A TRANSCRIPT?

Even after the report came out, President Trump continued his campaign of obstruction of justice. Rather than releasing a word-for-word transcript, of the kind the whistleblower referenced, Trump's administration released an edited transcript.

President Trump has claimed that this is "an exact transcript of my call, done by very talented people that do this — exact, word for word," but the White House's document itself says otherwise. "A Memorandum of a Telephone Conversation (TELCON) is not a verbatim transcript of a discussion," it reads. "The text in this document records the notes and recollections of Situation Room Duty officers and NSC policy staff assigned to listen and memorialize the conversation in written form as the conversation takes place."

There are also three sets of ellipses (". . .") in the transcript, which may be a sign that some of the conversation has been excised from the record. Trump officials have claimed that these ellipses merely serve as punctuation, meant to indicate a pause, but the *Washington Post* has reported that pauses in White House transcripts are traditionally punctuated with dashes rather than ellipses.

When Lt. Col. Vindman testified before Congress about President Trump's phone call, he confirmed the *Washington Post*'s reporting. Not only did the transcript contain key omissions — including additional discussion surrounding Vice President Biden and Burisma — but at least one of them was replaced by ellipses. And when Vindman attempted to change the transcript to more accurately reflect the conversation, his edits were rejected.

Either way, for the purposes of this article of impeachment, let's assume that despite all these red flags, the "transcript" is comprehensive. That still wouldn't affect the case, because the document President Trump released was itself massively incriminating. And just like Nixon's tapes, as I've explained, this "transcript" is only one element of a much larger story of obstruction of justice.

EXECUTIVE PRIVILEGE

Nixon didn't only suppress the smoking-gun tape. As laid out in Article III of his articles of impeachment, he also asserted executive privilege to deny Congress access to evidence — and to try to establish immunity not only from impeachment but from congressional oversight in general. That is exactly what President Trump is doing today.

Even before President Trump's call with Zelensky became public, Trump had adopted an unprecedented view of executive privilege. He asserted it to block Congress from obtaining documents about the census citizenship question, invoked it to try to bar the full Mueller report from being given to Congress, and used it to prevent his former White House counsel, Don McGahn, from providing documents to Congress — or from testifying before them.

As David Graham has argued in *The Atlantic,* Trump's interpretation of executive power often has a circular logic, which renders it impossible even to begin to hold him accountable. "In defending Trump, his attorneys have contended that Congress cannot obtain documents related to Trump's financial dealings, because that's a power reserved for prosecutors," Graham wrote. "Elsewhere, they have argued that prosecutors can't investigate Trump, because that's a power delegated to Congress under the Constitution. And when Congress has attempted to flex that impeachment power, Trump has said it's a coup, and that the only proper venue for presidential accountability is elections."

There's a simple way to understand this. Our founders created three "I's" to rein in a lawless president — indictment, investigation, and impeachment — and Trump's claim is that none of them apply to him.

On indictment, his attorney general, William Barr, has said that President Trump is shielded even from the 10 instances of obstruction of justice documented in the Mueller report because of DOJ memos, written during Nixon's and Clinton's presidencies, barring the indictment of a sitting president. The idea behind this guideline, to quote the DOJ, was that an indictment "would interfere with the President's unique official duties, most of which cannot be performed by anyone else." In other words, Nixon's and Clinton's Justice Departments believed that a criminal indictment would distract the president from doing his job. Trump's DOJ, of course, has taken the same approach. So the first I, "indictment," is out.

And yet — somehow, President Trump has taken the position that he cannot be investigated either, even though this claim flatly contradicts the very DOJ memos he relies on regarding indictment, which say he can in fact be investigated. So the second "I" is out too. And now President Trump is taking the view that he cannot be impeached and that the entire process is illegitimate and a coup. There goes the third "I" as well.

President Trump's claims of executive privilege may be particularly creative, but he is not the first president to push back against congressional oversight. Indeed, our constitutional system has always been defined by a balance between the public's need for transparency and the government's need to have a zone of secrecy around decision-making.

Both transparency and secrecy are important, but in many cases there's no avoiding the fact that they can be mutually exclusive. The Constitution, as written, erred on the side of transparency, with no mention whatsoever of executive privilege in its original text. But since it was ratified, presidents over time have found a need for their advisers to give them frank information without fear of embarrassment, and the privilege has been used by Democratic and Republican presidents alike — who have refused to provide certain documents and testimony in congressional investigations of various sorts.

Nixon differentiated himself from his predecessors, however, by adopting a particularly expansive understanding of executive privilege, viewing it as a license to ignore congressional oversight altogether. That is the philosophical underpinning of the infamous comment following his resignation: "When the president does it, that means that it is not illegal."

This belief, of course, had already been proven false by the time Nixon said it — when the Supreme Court ruled that he had to release the tapes. Which is why, for a while, Nixon's view of executive privilege seemed to be headed to the ash heap of history. When I teach constitutional law every year, my students are aghast at these Nixon arguments — because they don't only seem unconstitutional; if the stakes were not this high, they would almost be comical. Yet here we are in 2019, and Nixon is back. On steroids.

In the wake of Nixon's resignation, presidents were circumspect in their invocations of executive privilege, not wanting to be associated with Watergate. Presidents Gerald Ford, Jimmy Carter, and George H. W. Bush each invoked it only once, President Reagan three times. The exception was Bill Clinton, who used it over a dozen times. Ken Starr's impeachment referral to Congress actually enumerated this as a reason for impeachment, arguing that President Clinton had abused executive privilege, a referral that I believe (and argued at the time) had strength to it.

Clinton's use of executive privilege, to shield personal wrongdoing, had strong echoes of Mr. Nixon. And, for that reason, it attracted a lot of scrutiny — not only in Congress but also in the courts. Like Nixon, Clinton eventually had to choose between cooperating and obstructing justice. Unlike Nixon, he chose the former.

Presidents George W. Bush and Barack Obama saw Clinton's story as a cautionary tale — only invoking privilege sparingly (six times for Bush, one for Obama). But President Trump appears to be dead set on following the precedent set by Nixon and Clinton. This seemed to be true well before his phone call with Zelensky, but as soon as the House of Representatives opened its impeachment inquiry, Trump's interpretation of executive privilege became even more extreme, as he deployed the powers vested in him as president to obstruct justice.

"YOU'RE DAMN RIGHT WE'RE OBSTRUCTING"

Just over two weeks after Speaker Pelosi formally opened an impeachment inquiry, on October 8, US ambassador George Sondland, a key witness to President Trump's conduct with Ukraine, was set to testify before Congress. Texts sent to him by Ambassador Taylor — including the "it's crazy to withhold security assistance for help with a political campaign" text — were at the core of the case against President Trump. Sondland's response — including the "I believe you are incorrect about President Trump's intentions" text — was at the core of President Trump's defense. Many believed the phone call between President Trump and Sondland, which took place in the nearly five-hour window between the two texts, held answers to some of the most important questions about President Trump's arrangement with President Zelensky, and about his efforts to cover it up. Sondland's testimony, investigators had hoped, would provide some clarity.

But early in the morning of the very day on which Sondland was set to testify, the White House announced that he would be barred from doing so. Shortly thereafter, President Trump tweeted: "I would love to send Ambassador Sondland, a really good man and great American, to testify, but unfortunately he would be testifying before a totally compromised kangaroo court." That same day President Trump's White House counsel, Pat Cipollone, sent Congress the letter I mentioned in Chapter 2 (which is reproduced in the appendix), declaring, "President Trump cannot permit his Administration to participate in this partisan inquiry under these circumstances."

Cipollone's eight-page letter, as David Graham has argued, can be captured in a five-word phrase: "You're damn right we're obstructing."

As with Trump's previous claims of executive privilege, Cipollone's letter rests on a fundamental contradiction. On the one hand, Trump's lawyers have refused to participate in any criminal investigations because of their belief that the president cannot be indicted in court. The only way you can investigate a president, they argue, is through impeachment. On the other hand, President Trump's lawyers have begun arguing that impeachment itself is "illegitimate."

These two beliefs together would leave Congress with no way to compel the president to participate in their inquiry—in effect, rendering him above the law. That, it seems, is exactly the intention of President Trump's lawyers at the Justice Department. Indeed, they recently went so far as to tell US District Court chief judge Beryl Howell that they believed the Supreme Court ruling compelling Nixon to release his tapes may have been decided differently today.

Judge Howell's response to the Trump Administration? "Wow. Okay."

Our Constitution leaves us with two remedies for a president like this. The first is our courts. Whenever a president refuses to comply with a formal subpoena from Congress, the House can challenge his claims of executive privilege before a federal court in Washington, DC. If either party is unsatisfied with this ruling, they can challenge it at the Court of Appeals in Washington—and, if they are still unsatisfied, ultimately at the Supreme Court. That is exactly what happened in Watergate.

Many believe this time will be different, because the majority of justices on today's Supreme Court were appointed by Republican presidents. But the experience of President Nixon, who lost his case unanimously despite having nominated three of the justices who heard it, is instructive. The Supreme Court is composed of life-tenured justices precisely for moments such as this. And no one, particularly this president, should assume that politics will protect him in the highest court in the land.

The second remedy for a president like this is impeachment, regardless of whether the Supreme Court compels him to release additional evidence. Even without a single new piece of information, we already know with 100 percent certainty the answer to the question of whether or not he obstructed justice: yes. (And no matter what happens next, the answer to that question will be the same.)

We also know that this isn't the first time President Trump obstructed justice.

While none of Special Counsel Mueller's findings need to be (or even, for that matter, should be) included in the articles of impeachment against President Trump, they do provide us with more evidence that President Trump is likely to obstruct justice again. After all, he obstructed Mueller's investigation not once, not twice, but at least ten times.

He asked FBI director James Comey to "see [his] way clear to letting [the investigation into Michael] Flynn go." When Comey refused, he fired him — later telling Russian officials he had faced "great pressure because of Russia," which had been "taken off" by Comey's removal. He asked his lawyer, Don McGahn, to fire Special Counsel Mueller as well — a request McGahn refused to carry out, according to Mueller, "deciding he would rather resign than trigger what he regarded as a potential Saturday Night Massacre." He edited a statement from his son Donald Trump, Jr., about the Trump Tower meeting and then lied about it. He intimidated witnesses, calling on Michael Cohen to "stay strong" and saying he believed "flipping . . . almost ought to be outlawed." He tried to convince his attorney general, Jeff Sessions, to "unrecuse" himself from the case, telling aides he wanted Sessions to "protect" him. And on and on and on.

President Trump may not have colluded with Russia, but he did all he could to impede and bring an end to the investigation into whether or not he did. And he got away with it only because he played his DOJ "get-out-of-jail-free card," with Mueller stymied by the notion that a sitting president could not be indicted.

Now, as I've explained, President Trump's conduct with Ukraine would be impeachable even if he had cooperated fully with the Mueller investigation — indeed, even if Russia had never interfered in the 2016 presidential election. But what Mueller's report shows is that President Trump believes he can obstruct justice with impunity.

And with Ukraine, by "locking down" the whistleblower report; by saying that the whistleblower should be treated like a "spy"; by refusing to comply with subpoenas from Congress; by claiming Adam Schiff, his principal investigator, should be "arrested for treason"; by calling the impeachment probe a "coup"; and by trying to block witnesses, like Sondland, from testifying, Trump is using the same playbook to obstruct justice once again.

The only question is whether, this time, we'll do anything about it.

The Bottom Line

Here's the bottom line: President Trump asked President Zelensky of Ukraine to investigate Vice President Biden. He solicited bribes. He covered up what he did. And he has refused to participate in the impeachment inquiry against him, depriving Congress of its constitutionally guaranteed authority — and indeed responsibility — to investigate the executive branch.

In committing these acts, he clearly is guilty of three high crimes:

1. Abusing the public trust by soliciting foreign interference in the 2020 presidential election;
2. Abusing the public trust by engaging in bribery — repeatedly — through his quid pro quo exchanges with President Zelensky of Ukraine;
3. Abusing the public trust by obstructing justice in the investigations of his conduct, adopting an unconstitutional view of executive power.

We have all the evidence we need to prove the underlying high crime of soliciting foreign interference. The evidence on bribery, too, is open-and-shut — so much so that the president's acting chief of staff at one point confessed to it. And we have all the evidence we need to prove the cover-up. What's more, President Trump has clearly stated that he will not stop asking foreign powers to help him win elections — unless we remove him.

Which is why we must.

As John Dean, President Nixon's counsel, said during Watergate, "There is a cancer on the presidency, and cancers, if not removed, only grow." Congress must use the authority granted to it by our Constitution to remove that cancer now, before it's too late.

4

QUESTIONS AND ANSWERS

The facts are clear. President Trump wielded the powers of the presidency for the benefit of himself instead of for the benefit of the American people. He solicited foreign interference in our elections — and, in the process, jeopardized our national security by leaving himself vulnerable to blackmail. He proposed not one but at least two quid pro quo exchanges to President Zelensky. He has obstructed justice into the investigations of his conduct, adopting an unconstitutional view of executive power. And he has promised to do it all again.

No matter what new developments take place — as many surely will, even between the writing of this book and its arrival in your hands — these facts will not change. But you may still have questions about the process. Like: What does the Constitution say about impeachment? (Surprisingly, not very much.) If the House votes to impeach, does the Senate have to hold hearings? (Probably.) Can Congress send President Trump to prison? (No, but if he's removed, courts can.)

The first half of this chapter is devoted to answering these kinds of logistical questions about impeachment.

The second half of the chapter, meanwhile, focuses on answering questions specifically related to the Ukraine case and responding to the most common arguments you might hear from President Trump's defenders. Like: Didn't Hunter Biden commit crimes? (No, but that doesn't make what he did right.) Isn't the case against President Trump based in hearsay? (No.) And why can't we wait until the 2020 election? (Because Trump has promised to cheat to win it.)

Most of these questions have been covered in the preceding chapters, so if you see one you already know the answer to, feel free to skip ahead. But I want you to have an analysis of the flaws in President Trump's most common defenses all in one place, so if you're in the middle of an argument about impeachment with your uncle, you'll know where to look.

Of course, none of the answers to these questions are essential to understanding the case for impeachment, so if you want to skip this chapter entirely, Godspeed. But if you have any loose ends you want tied up, or any questions you want answered, this chapter is for you. And if there's anything I haven't covered, you can ask me on Twitter via @neal_katyal.

Process Questions

Process Question #1: What does the Constitution say about impeachment?

> *Article I, Section 2, Clause 5: "The House of Representatives . . . shall have the sole Power of Impeachment."*

This means only the House can begin impeachment proceedings against a president before a trial can occur in the Senate. It does not, however, mean the House can *remove* a president on its own. That requires the Senate. Impeachment, as defined in Clause 5, is merely the formal *accusation*.

Think of the House's role as charging a defendant (like a grand jury) and the Senate's role as serving as the jury. Even if the members of the House think a crime has been committed, they cannot convict, since that's the role of the Senate. And even if the senators are convinced that a high crime took place, they cannot initiate removal proceedings unless the House first brings them the accusation in the form of a referral of what are called "articles of impeachment."

> *Article I, Section 3, Clauses 6 and 7: "The Senate shall have the sole Power to try all Impeachments. When sitting for that Purpose, they shall be on Oath or Affirmation. When the President of the United States is tried, the Chief Justice shall preside: And no Person shall be convicted without the Concurrence of two-thirds of members present. The judgment in Cases of Impeachment shall not extend further than to removal from Office, and disqualification to hold*

and enjoy any Office of honor, Trust or Profit under the
United States; but the Party convicted shall nevertheless be
liable and subject to Indictment, Trial, Judgment and Pun-
ishment, according to Law."

These clauses can be distilled to a few key points:

1. As mentioned above, the Senate ultimately determines
   whether or not a president should be convicted. Only if
   two-thirds of the senators agree with the verdict can the
   commander in chief be removed from office.
2. The Senate can't sentence the president to anything other
   than "removal from Office" and disqualification from future
   officeholding. Most importantly, it can't send him to prison.
3. Impeachment proceedings in the Senate are presided over
   by the chief justice of the United States. (More on what this
   means later.)

   Article II, Section 4: "The President, Vice President, and
   all civil Officers of the United States, shall be removed from
   Office on Impeachment for, and Conviction of, Treason,
   Bribery, or other high Crimes and Misdemeanors."

There are two takeaways from this section: you can be impeached only for a high crime or misdemeanor (defined in Chapter 1 and below), and you can be impeached only if you're a president, vice president, or civil officer. Historically, the term "civil
officer" has mostly stood in for judges, who make up 15 of the
19 cases of impeachment in US history. Other presidential appointees, like cabinet members, are also subject to impeachment.

Representatives and senators, on the other hand, do not qualify as "civil Officers of the United States."

> *Article II, Section 2: The president "shall have power to grant reprieves and pardons for offenses against the United States, except in cases of impeachment."*

This clause ensures the president cannot pardon himself or one of his appointees if they are impeached by Congress.

Process Question #2: How does impeachment actually work?

The Constitution provides sparse guidance on how to impeach a president; instead, many of the protocols have been determined by Congress over the last two centuries. And some are still being figured out.

But we do have a *sense* of how impeachment works. After all, the procedures the Senate used for the impeachment of President Clinton were by and large the same ones they adopted for the impeachment of President Johnson more than a century earlier. And in all likelihood, President Trump's impeachment would be conducted in a similar fashion.

Impeachment, as the Constitution demands, begins in the House of Representatives, where members of Congress decide whether they believe the president should be charged with a high crime or misdemeanor. This is generally determined in committees, but *which* committees it's determined by is less clear.

The House Judiciary Committee can run the investigation, as it did during Nixon's impeachment, or the House can establish a new committee solely for the purpose of impeachment. The House can also move straight into drafting articles of impeachment if the representatives don't think an investigation is necessary.

Once articles of impeachment are drafted, they tend to be voted on by the investigatory committee before they are put to the entire House. (They can be voted on individually or all at once.) If the majority of the House votes to impeach for any of the articles, the case is sent to the Senate for trial.

When articles arrive in the Senate, per Article I, Section 3, Clause 6 of the Constitution, senators take a special oath to "do impartial justice according to the Constitution and the laws." With the chief justice of the United States presiding, senators hear arguments from both sides. The case *for* impeachment is made by "managers" who are appointed by the House of Representatives. The case *against* impeachment is made by the president's lawyers. The chief justice is in charge of deciding what is and isn't admissible evidence, but if a majority of senators disagree with his ruling, he can be overruled.

After all the evidence has been presented, the Senate votes on each article of impeachment individually. As law professor Charles Black wrote, every senator is "registering his best judgment 'on the facts' and 'on the law.' That means that he is answering two questions together: 'Did the president do what he is charged in this Article with having done?' [And] if he did, did that action constitute an impeachable offense within the meaning of the constitutional phrase?"

If fewer than 67 senators answer both of those questions "yes," the president is acquitted. On the other hand, if 67 senators rule the president guilty of *even one of the articles,* he is convicted. The exclusive punishments for conviction, as indicated in Article I,

Section 3, Clause 6, are removal from office and disqualification from future officeholding.

Process Question #3: What rights does President Trump have during the impeachment process? Is President Trump within his rights to refuse to take the stand?

Impeachment is not governed by the same rules as our courts, which means defendants are not guaranteed all of the same rights before Congress that they have in criminal proceedings. In fact, nowhere in the Constitution are defendants in impeachment proceedings expressly provided with rights of any kind.

That didn't stop President Nixon from trying to avoid participating in his impeachment inquiry. As I described in Chapters 1 and 3, he refused to comply with subpoenas and declined to cooperate with the inquiry. That in itself became the focus of Article III of his impeachment. To quote Senator Lindsey Graham, as I did in Chapter 3, "The day Richard Nixon failed to answer that subpoena is the day he was subject to impeachment because he took the power of Congress over the impeachment process away from Congress and became the judge and jury." That's why, despite Trump's protestations, the president must respect subpoenas from Congress — and he certainly cannot decline to "participate" altogether, as his lawyer has suggested Trump plans to do.

But must he appear and testify under oath? The answer to that question turns on whether Trump has a "privilege" he can cite to avoid testifying.

A privilege is simply a legal right to keep certain information confidential, even when faced with questions in court. And there are many kinds of privileges in our justice system, from executive privilege, which I discussed in detail in Chapter 3, to spousal privilege, which protects husbands and wives from having to reveal information about each other.

But just because there are lots of kinds of privileges does not mean that they are successfully invoked very often. In fact, the American legal system generally believes that people have rights to other folks' evidence, so privileges are narrowly construed.

The privilege germane to this question is the right to avoid self-incrimination. In ordinary criminal trials, presidents, like all Americans, can cite this privilege, as the Fifth Amendment bars forcing anyone to self-incriminate. But there is no express privilege in the Constitution that protects the president from being compelled to participate in an impeachment proceeding.

Now, one can imagine the president's lawyers making an argument that goes like this: "I don't have a privilege in the impeachment context, but I do in the criminal context, so if I give testimony in the impeachment context, it could be used one day in a criminal trial. That means that even in cases of impeachment, I still have Fifth Amendment protections against self-incrimination."

There are many problems with that argument, starting with the fact that Congress could agree to bar the president's testimony in a future criminal proceeding if a credible argument could later be made to a judge that due process requires that exclusion. It would also, of course, be a hard argument for President Trump to make, because he'd essentially be admitting his criminal guilt. And he'd be doing something federal employees are generally not permitted to do.

After all, unlike with civilians, we expect our federal employees to tell the truth to law enforcement, rather than hide behind their privileges — because our safety depends on their transparency.

That's true of the lowest-ranking members of our government; and it's certainly true of our most important federal employee, the president of the United States.

Process Question #4: What is the role of the House? Will it call witnesses, including Trump?

The role of the House is to investigate the president's conduct and determine whether or not to charge him in the form of articles of impeachment — which means, as part of its duties as the investigatory body, the House can call witnesses.

But the president cannot easily be compelled to testify under oath. In fact, according to Andy Wright, President Barack Obama's associate counsel in the White House, only three sitting US presidents have ever testified before Congress, even outside the context of an impeachment inquiry: George Washington, Abraham Lincoln, and Gerald Ford. (At least one other president, Woodrow Wilson, also answered questions from Congress, but he did so at the White House, not on Capitol Hill.)

The reason so few presidents have testified outside the impeachment context is that they can cite any number of privileges to avoid answering questions under oath, from the privilege against self-incrimination to executive privilege — and stall as those claims are litigated in court. But as I explained in response to Process Question #3, when it comes to removing a president, these arguments often don't pass muster, since impeachment is not a criminal proceeding. And if President Trump tried to make them, he would face the very difficult political reality of looking like he is afraid to testify and incriminate himself.

That hasn't stopped President Trump from *trying* to decline to participate in the inquiry altogether, but as I explained in Chapter 3, his lawyers' arguments simply don't stand up to scrutiny. President Trump, like President Nixon, will ultimately be compelled to honor subpoenas — and comply with any formal requests for information from the House — or be held accountable for the lawless refusal to do so, perhaps ultimately through the impeachment process itself. After all, Article III of President Nixon's impeachment centered on his refusal to comply with subpoenas.

Executive privilege, like any privilege, is generally narrowly defined because our system recognizes an overwhelming need for the public to have access to information. But President Trump's stonewalling, and in particular his invocation of executive privilege, suffers from another serious legal problem: himself.

All privileges are subject to something called a "waiver," the idea being that if you air confidential information in public, it's no longer, well, confidential. In a sense, this is self-evident, but we've also never had a president who has so casually waived his privilege. That's what's ironic about President Trump's lawyers' claims of sweeping executive privilege: Trump endlessly tweets about the very events that are the subject of the inquiries. It was his choice, after all, to disclose the July 25 "transcript," and it was his acting chief of staff, Mick Mulvaney, who decided to admit a quid pro quo. I understand why his team might not like the result of all his disclosures, but they can't yell backsies now. It's too late. And the House is going to get all the evidence related to the disclosures President Trump has made publicly.

Once the House has conducted a comprehensive investigation, with or without the president's participation, members draft articles of impeachment and then vote on them. Historically, the Judiciary Committee has voted on the articles first, before they have been sent to the full House for a final vote.

The House's role in impeachment doesn't end there. When the Senate holds a trial on the articles, representatives of the House serve as the prosecutors, presenting the case for impeachment.

Process Question #5: What does the Senate do? What does the trial look like?

As soon as the House votes on the articles of impeachment, every senator must swear a special oath, promising to do "impartial justice according to the Constitution and the laws." Only once they have done so can the Senate transform into a tribunal.

After the senators take their oath, they hear arguments from the prosecution ("managers" appointed by the House) and from the defense (the president's lawyers). The chief justice presides over the trial, because the vice president, who normally presides over trials in the Senate, has a clear conflict of interest. But in the end, even though the chief justice is tasked with making some decisions (like determining what evidence is admissible, as mentioned earlier), senators are the judge and jury. Indeed, they can even overrule the chief justice's decisions by a majority vote.

As Chief Justice William Rehnquist wrote in a letter after presiding over President Clinton's impeachment: "On several occasions when asked what I did at the trial . . . I took a leaf out of [the opera] *Iolanthe* and replied, 'I did nothing in particular, and did it very well.'"

Once the senators and the chief justice have heard all the arguments, they vote on each of the articles of impeachment individually. If 67 senators rule the president guilty on even one of the counts, the president is immediately removed from office.

Process Question #6: Does the Senate have to hold a trial?

Yes, according to the Senate's own rules.

The rulebook reads: "Upon [articles of impeachment] being presented to the Senate, the Senate shall, at 1 o'clock afternoon of the day (Sunday excepted) following such presentation, or sooner if ordered by the Senate, proceed to the consideration of such articles and shall continue in session from day to day (Sundays excepted) after the trial shall commence (unless otherwise ordered by the Senate) until final judgment shall be rendered."

This language indicates that the Senate has no choice but to conduct a trial. And that's exactly what they did when the House sent them articles of impeachment in the cases of President Johnson and President Clinton.

But Senator Mitch McConnell, who is the majority leader of the Senate, could very well disregard this practice. After all, in defiance of precedent, he didn't even hold a hearing for President Obama's Supreme Court nominee, Merrick Garland. And while the Constitution says that the Senate "shall have the sole power to try" a president, it never quite specifies that the body must exercise that power. The word "shall" there modifies the word "power," not the word "try"; in other words, it's saying that *only* the Senate can hold a trial to remove a president, not that the Senate is ordered to do so.

The good news is: Senator McConnell has stated that if the House voted to impeach President Trump, he "would have no choice but to take it up." But he added, "How long you're on it is a whole different matter." With this statement, Senator McConnell seems to be implying that he might rush the impeachment process — and I wouldn't rule out the possibility of his trying to change the Senate rules to avoid taking up impeachment entirely.

As McConnell wrote in a fundraising pitch, "The way that impeachment stops is a Senate majority with me as majority leader."

He concluded: "Please contribute before the deadline."

For Senator McConnell to try to block the evidence from being carefully heard and considered would be a profound dereliction of his job. He would go down in history as one of the most anti-democratic people ever to have served in the United States government. Our founders put the two-thirds voting requirement for removal from office in the Constitution precisely to avoid stunts like this, because they assumed that leaders like Senator McConnell would trust the process and accept that if, after a trial, 67 senators believed the president committed a high crime, then the evidence must be strong enough to prove him guilty. Senator McConnell should let the process unfold and see where the evidence leads. It is his constitutional duty to do no less.

Process Question #7: What level of certainty is needed for the Senate to convict the president?

In criminal cases, a defendant can be convicted only if there's evidence "beyond a reasonable doubt." That means the jury has to be very sure, far more than 50 percent, that a defendant is guilty.

In civil cases, by contrast, a defendant can be convicted with a "preponderance of evidence," which is interpreted to be any level of certainty greater than 50 percent.

Impeachment is a difficult case because it's neither a criminal nor a civil trial — and nowhere in the Constitution can senators find guidance on what level of certainty they need to convict.

As law professor Charles Black argues, "Overwhelming preponderance of the evidence . . . comes as close as present legal language can to denoting the desired standard." But ultimately this is a choice left to each and every senator to decide for themselves.

Process Question #8: What happens after a president is removed?

Once the president is removed, the Senate has to decide whether to take a separate vote to disqualify him from holding office again.

The immediate consequence of the president's removal, whether a disqualification vote takes place or not, is that the vice president then swears an oath of office and assumes the role of president of the United States. He is also entitled to appoint a vice president of his own, who becomes next in line to the presidency.

After he completes the prior president's term, he can choose to run for reelection, and if he wins, he can run for reelection once again. He can also, of course, decline to seek another term.

If for some reason the vice president is impeached alongside the president, the next person in line to the presidency is the Speaker of the House.

Process Question #9: How long does impeachment take?

Who knows? There are no requirements for how long impeachment takes (except of course for the implied deadline of the next presidential election). In the past, impeachment inquiries have ranged in length from Johnson's impeachment, which took only three days, to Nixon's, which lasted a full eight months.

Speaker Pelosi and congressional leadership have reportedly indicated that they would like to move this process along in as efficient a manner as possible, especially given how soon the 2020 presidential election will take place.

Process Question #10: Can federal courts block an unfair impeachment?

No, Congress has the final word.

Walter Nixon was a federal judge in the 1980s with an unfortunate last name. This became especially true when he was impeached and convicted in 1989 for lying to a grand jury and for bringing disrepute on the federal judiciary. Nixon, believing that he hadn't been tried fairly, attempted to challenge his impeachment in court. His case ended up in the highest court in the land — where the Supreme Court ruled that "the Judiciary, and the Supreme Court in particular, were not chosen to have any role in impeachments."

This is in line with what's in the Constitution, but it's also simple common sense. Imagine if a president, after being impeached and convicted, brought an appeal of sorts to the Supreme Court, which then put "the impeached and convicted president back in for the rest of his term," wrote law professor Charles Black. "I don't think I possess the resources of rhetoric adequate to characterizing the absurdity of that position."

Of course, if a president is indicted after he leaves office, courts, including federal courts, are charged with making the final determination as to whether he is guilty of whatever crimes are laid out in his indictment. That's another reason that the Supreme Court in the Walter Nixon case found federal courts could not have a role in impeachment: "The Framers recognized that most likely there would be two sets of proceedings for individuals who commit impeachable offenses: the impeachment trial and a separate criminal trial," the Court wrote. "In fact, the Constitution explicitly provides for two separate proceedings . . . The Framers deliberately separated the two forums to avoid raising the specter of bias and to ensure independent judgments."

Process Question #11: What is an impeachable offense?

As discussed at length in Chapter 1, an impeachable offense is defined by our Constitution as "treason, bribery, or other high crimes and misdemeanors." Simple, right?

Well, no, because the precise definition of "high crimes and misdemeanors" was never determined by our founders. And the two most commonsense understandings of the phrase are wrong. High crimes and misdemeanors are not necessarily crimes as defined by criminal codes (after all, if the president decided to nuke Canada unprovoked, that would technically be within his rights as commander in chief but would nonetheless be grounds for impeachment). Nor do all crimes listed in criminal codes qualify as high crimes and misdemeanors (one of the two high crimes enumerated by our founders, bribery, wasn't even in criminal codes when the Constitution was written).

But based on discussions at the Constitutional Convention, based on the legal usage of the word "high," and based on precedent, constitutional scholars have come to something of a consensus as to the definition of high crimes and misdemeanors, which I've summarized as follows:

> *High crimes and misdemeanors are abuses of public trust,*
> *in which the president wields the powers of his office to*
> *serve himself at the expense of the people he represents.*

To quote Vice President Mike Pence, "This business of high crimes and misdemeanors goes to the question of whether or not the person serving as President of the United States put their own interests, their personal interests, ahead of public service."

In *Federalist No. 65*, Alexander Hamilton provided a similar definition for impeachable offenses, defining them as "those offenses which proceed from . . . the abuse or violation of some public trust . . . as they relate chiefly to injuries done immediately to the society itself." This is the definition I've adopted throughout this book.

Process Question #12: What does it mean to be a whistleblower? What rights and protections are they afforded?

Whistleblowers are members of an organization who observe wrongdoing and receive protection in exchange for revealing it.

As I wrote in Chapter 2, inspired by America's first whistleblowers, Samuel Shaw and Richard Marven, our country has had protections for whistleblowers in place since 1778 — nearly a decade before the Constitution was written. Throughout the more than 240 years since, whistleblowers have enjoyed largely bipartisan support.

When I was fighting the MacLean whistleblower case, as I noted in Chapter 2, a bipartisan group in Congress, including Senator Chuck Grassley and Representative Darrell Issa, came together to tell the Supreme Court that "whistleblowers play a vital role in Congressional oversight of the federal bureaucracy." They concluded: "Congress thus relies on individuals working within agencies to supply the information it needs to guard the public purse and give effect to the checks and balances that are essential to the separation of powers. By blowing the whistle, those individuals perform an invaluable public service."

President Obama and Congress built on existing whistleblower protections to devise policies designed specifically to protect executive-branch whistleblowers in the intelligence community and ensure they would not become victims of retaliation for disclosing information. That way, if anyone saw misconduct in the executive branch, they would feel free to report it.

By contrast, President Trump called the whistleblower in the Ukraine matter "close to a spy" and suggested that "in the old days" spies were "handled" differently. (For context, as I've noted, they were executed.)

Process Question #13: Should we expect the whistleblower to come forward and reveal their identity if they want us to take their allegations seriously?

No. Whistleblowing is designed to be an anonymous process — which is why, under existing laws, the inspector general may not disclose a whistleblower's identity without that person's consent. In fact, the director of national intelligence revealed during his testimony before the House Intelligence Committee that even he does not know the identity of the whistleblower.

There's a clear reason for this: even with the legal protections in place, whistleblowers are often punished when their identities are revealed. In some cases, they are fired or demoted. In others, they are forced out of government entirely. I can tell you from defending whistleblowers that it is a lonely existence. You lose some of your friends and possibly even your family. It's typically much easier to keep your head down and mind your own business.

This whistleblower, in particular, has special reasons to fear being outed, since the president has launched a series of personal attacks against them, saying that they should be "exposed" and "questioned," accusing them of being a partisan, labeling them a "spy," and saying that we should "handle" them "like we did in the old days," a comment many, as I've noted, believed was a reference to execution.

The whistleblower may very well reveal who they are, but with attacks like these coming from the most powerful human being on earth, I understand why the individual would feel safer without being identified and exposed on television, in newspapers, and on social media.

Process Question #14: Can the president be sent to prison through impeachment?

Yes and no. The Senate cannot issue any sentence other than removing the president from office, but once he has been removed, he is just a regular citizen of the United States and subject to the same laws as everyone else. So if he is charged with a crime and convicted of it after leaving office, he can indeed go to prison. In fact, the Department of Justice memos that preclude the indictment of a sitting president, mentioned in Chapter 3, expressly say that once a president has been impeached, he is subject to criminal prosecution. This could come in the form of a federal criminal prosecution or even a state criminal prosecution, and reporting indicates that various state governments are already investigating individuals and entities associated with Trump. (For instance: Trump seems to be an unindicted co-conspirator, aka "Individual No. 1," in the Southern District of New York's campaign finance charges against the president's former lawyer Michael Cohen.)

There is a caveat, however: the pardon power. A president can't pardon himself if the Senate rules him guilty of an impeachable offense, because Article II forbids pardons in cases of impeachment. But his successor *can* pardon him with respect to criminal activity, and we have an example of that. In an attempt to bring about unity after President Nixon's impeachment, President Ford pardoned his predecessor. That means that President Trump could very well be pardoned for any crimes he's guilty of by a subsequent president — perhaps even before he's been charged with such crimes. Of course, that would not inure him to prosecution for any crimes he may commit after the pardon.

Process Question #15: What punishments are available in impeachment?

The Constitution strictly defines the punishments the Senate can mete out in Article I: "Judgment in Cases of Impeachment shall not extend further than to removal from Office, and disqualification to hold and enjoy any Office of honor, Trust or Profit under the United States; but the Party convicted shall nevertheless be liable and subject to Indictment, Trial, Judgment and Punishment, according to Law."

This means three things. First, impeachment proceedings will generally center on removal from office. That's the usual focus of impeachment. But they also permit the Senate to add a further punishment of disqualifying someone from holding future office. In other words, the Senate can decide whether it is strictly removing a president from office once or whether to bar him from ever running for elected office again.

Second, because the Constitution enumerates these two tracks of punishment for an impeached official, but doesn't instruct the Senate on how far to go in applying them, there are interesting strategies the Senate can use. The senators could, for instance, remove Trump from office but not bar him from running again — saying in effect that if he really believes a new election will vindicate him, he can go ahead and give it his best shot. Or they could decide not to remove him from office now but disqualify him from ever running again. Neither of these possibilities makes much logical sense, given the strength of the case against him, but then again, we are talking about Washington, DC.

Third, the "shall not extend further than" language in Article I means that criminal punishments are off the table for the Senate. (This was more extensively discussed in response to the previous question.) An impeached president can be subject to criminal indictment, but only if he's been removed from office by the Senate. And the prosecutors, as in any criminal case, would have to prove their case not in Congress but beyond a reasonable doubt in a court of law.

Case Questions

Case Question #1: Why can't we wait until the next election?

Because President Trump has demonstrated over and over again that he will do everything in his power — legal and illegal — to manipulate the results of the election in his favor, even if that means working with a foreign power to undermine our democracy.

As I argue in Chapter 1, when Trump asks Americans to wait until the election for a chance to remove him from office, it's like a cardshark asking to resolve a dispute with a game of blackjack when the very crime he's been accused of committing is cheating at blackjack.

The reason we can't wait until the election is that there's no guarantee President Trump won't try again to use the powers vested in him to rig it. (He already has.) Which is why we're left with no choice but to impeach him now.

As I detailed in Chapter 1, this is precisely the argument our founders had at the Constitutional Convention in Philadelphia. At first, Gouverneur Morris was unconvinced that impeachment needed to be in the Constitution — because he believed that re-election provided an adequate check on the president's power. "In case he should be re-elected, that will be sufficient proof of his innocence," he argued. Sound familiar?

But Morris's point was met with an immediate rejoinder by George Mason, which is one of the epigraphs of this book: "Shall any man be above Justice?" Mason asked. "Shall the man who has practiced corruption and by that means procured his appointment in the first instance, be suffered to escape punishment by repeating his guilt?"

In other words, without the protection of impeachment, what would stop a president from committing crimes to win office — particularly if he got away with it before and could "repeat his guilt" — when he knew he would have full immunity afterward?

By the end of the day, Mason — as well as James Madison and Benjamin Franklin — had convinced the majority of the convention that impeachment should in fact be in the Constitution. Even Gouvernour Morris came around. To quote the minutes from the July 20, 1787, meeting: "Mr. Govr. Morris admits corruption and some few other offenses to be such as ought to be impeachable."

The "wait for the next election" response was rejected by our 1787 founders, and it makes even less sense today.

The House launched its inquiry more than a year before the election; this isn't exactly a last-minute investigation. Indeed, every passing day is one in which President Trump could sell out the 2020 election to foreign interests, which would do untold damage to our democracy on Election Day. And, in the interim, we risk leaving a man in office — in charge of our treasury and our armed forces — who has shown disregard for the rule of law.

I'm not saying it's ever right to hurry into impeachment. Rather, I'm saying we don't have the option of waiting. The case is ripe. The time is now.

Case Question #2: How many articles of impeachment should we expect? Will they include charges related to the Mueller investigation?

Impeachments can be broad or narrow. In a broad impeachment inquiry, Congress enumerates each and every one of the president's high crimes and lists each as a separate article of impeachment. Such inquiries are meant to communicate the *breadth* of the president's high crimes.

In a narrow impeachment inquiry, articles of impeachment include only a few high crimes, which serve as buckets into which the president's various offenses are distributed. These inquiries are meant to communicate the *severity* of individual crimes.

Some legal scholars and members of Congress have made broad claims for impeaching President Trump, which makes sense, since he appears to be guilty of a number of high crimes. But if Congress is going to effectively make the case against him, its articles of impeachment cannot seem like a jumble of grievances. As Tribe and Matz write, "The Impeachment Clause directs attention to *particular* misdeeds, not the ambient badness of a presidency."

That's why I believe President Trump's impeachment should be the narrow variety, because for all the further wrongdoing that has come out about President Trump, as I enumerated in Chapter 3, his conduct with Ukraine alone provides Congress with more than sufficient evidence and offense for impeachment. What's more, I believe that expanding the articles to include activity not related to Ukraine would risk clouding the issue and leave President Trump an opening for a defense.

I've seen this firsthand at the Supreme Court, where advocates often mistakenly load up open-and-shut cases with all sorts of arguments they don't need to win. If the Court doubts even one of a lawyer's tangential claims, it will immediately look upon the core argument with suspicion, no matter how cut-and-dried a case it might be. This is less a legal issue than a psychological one.

There is no doubt that if Congress tried to charge the behavior in the Mueller report, for example, Trump would levy his standard tropes, from his claims that the investigation was a "witch hunt" to his (baseless) declaration of complete exoneration after Attorney General Barr "summarized" the report. So by expanding impeachment to include Mueller, Democrats would risk their core argument being overlooked — or distorted.

But it's also true that President Trump's behavior with Ukraine isn't unrelated to the Mueller investigation. In both cases, he solicited foreign election interference and covered it up. And even if President Trump didn't coordinate with Russia in the same way as he did with Ukraine, Mueller's report still paints a picture of a president who is willing to seek help from any quarter (including foreign governments); who disrespects and refuses to cooperate with law enforcement inquiries; and who tries to cover his tracks.

Although Congress could theoretically exclude all of that conduct from their articles of impeachment — and still have enough evidence to convict — they would be leaving the jury, and US citizens, with incomplete information. Moreover, in 100 years, people will read the articles of impeachment, and they may not really read much else. Shouldn't the articles document the full pattern of wrongdoing?

Fortunately, we don't have to choose between embracing the kind of narrow case that would be most effective and ignoring the Mueller report entirely, as the precedent of President Nixon's impeachment reveals. Instead of charging Nixon with a laundry list of offenses, the House Judiciary Committee adopted only three articles of impeachment. The main text of each article centered on Watergate, but the supporting paragraphs brought in other, well, Nixonian behavior.

Take, for example, Article I, which concerned obstruction of justice. The main text detailed the unlawful entry into Watergate by CREEP, as it related to Nixon's "plan designed to delay, impede, and obstruct the investigation of such illegal entry; to cover up, conceal, and protect those responsible; and to conceal the existence and scope of other unlawful covert activities." But the committee didn't stop there. The article had nine more paragraphs outlining a laundry list of offenses, ranging from misuse of the CIA to perjury. None of that, strictly speaking, was necessary at all to show the Watergate counts. But its inclusion helped tell the story — not just for the moment, but also for generations to come — of a president who believed he was above the law. After all, when Congress writes impeachment articles, it is writing them for the case at hand but also for history.

I think Congress should take a similar approach here. Instead of separating out every single offense in a different article, the House should group them into three articles, each of which would focus on a distinct high crime. In Chapter 3, I categorized these abuses of trust as "soliciting foreign interference," "bribery," and "obstruction of justice."

Each article should center on Ukraine, but as I demonstrated in Chapter 3, it is perfectly appropriate for Congress to include some of the strongest non-Ukraine behavior as supporting evidence.

Case Question #3: Was there a quid pro quo in this case?

As I explain in Chapter 3, a quid pro quo is not at all needed to impeach a president for bribery. But as it happens, during his phone call with President Zelensky, President Trump made at least two such offers.

The first came when President Zelensky mentioned military assistance from the United States, prompting President Trump to say, "I would like you to do us a favor though."

This is as simple a case as you will find: President Zelensky asked for something (Javelin missiles). President Trump in turn asked for a "favor." That's the definition of a quid pro quo exchange. In a quarter century of being a lawyer, I've never seen a documentation like this. Normally criminals are careful to avoid putting such things in writing.

The second quid pro quo between President Trump and President Zelensky was the exchange of an investigation into Vice President Biden for a visit to the White House. As discussed in Chapters 2 and 3, in advance of the call, Ambassador Volker wrote in a text: "Heard from the White House. Assuming President Z convinces Trump he will investigate . . . we will nail down his visit to Washington." On the call itself, in direct response to Zelensky's pledge to "work on the investigation," Trump said, "Whenever you would like to come to the White House, feel free to call." That is once again about as blatant a quid pro quo as you will find.

But don't just take it from me; many people in Trump's own administration understood the president to have been engaging in a quid pro quo too. As Ambassador Taylor, Trump's envoy to Ukraine, said in a text, "I think it's crazy to withhold security assistance for help with a political campaign." And acting White House chief of staff Mick Mulvaney confessed to the quid pro quo as well.

Taylor wasn't the only one who understood the scheme President Trump had been trying to pull off. According to extensive reporting, so did high-ranking officials from across the government, who were worried about this call in advance because they knew President Trump would propose the very quid pro quo he ultimately pursued. And clearly, White House officials knew that what had taken place on the call was wrong — because they did everything they could to cover it up.

Case Question #4: If there wasn't a quid pro quo, would President Trump have committed an impeachable offense?

For the sake of argument, let's pretend President Trump hadn't pursued a quid pro quo of any kind with President Zelensky. Would his behavior still warrant impeachment? The answer is yes. He would be committing a cardinal sin according to our founders — seeking assistance from a foreign government in taking down one of his political opponents. Moreover, in asking Ukraine to deliver on a request for him — one that would embarrass President Trump if it were ever to become public — he would be providing President Zelensky with tremendous leverage over him.

As I noted in Chapter 2, Ukraine could have said to President Trump, "If you don't double our aid, or triple it, or quadruple it, then I'll tell the American people you asked for our help, the help of a foreign government, in your election." To avoid the appearance of impropriety, President Trump would be left with little choice but to accede to that demand.

That's why even if Ukraine totally refused to honor Trump's request, his actions would still warrant impeachment — because suddenly, in addition to serving the American people, our president would also be forced to oblige the will of Ukraine. That's an abuse of public trust, and it's reason alone for impeachment, even in the absence of an explicit quid pro quo.

Case Question #5: Is the case against President Trump grounded in hearsay? Is that illegal?

In the days after the whistleblower's report was released, President Trump's allies began decrying it as "hearsay."

Lindsey Graham, in a tweet referenced in Chapter 2, wrote: "In America you can't even get a parking ticket based on hearsay testimony. But you can impeach a president? I certainly hope not." Shortly thereafter, President Trump adopted this argument himself, arguing that the whistleblower's report was all based on second- and thirdhand sources.

This would ordinarily be a strong defense, but there was a big problem: the call summary released by President Trump himself on the day prior to the White House's declassification of the complaint confirmed the lion's share of the whistleblower's allegations. Many of the rest of the whistleblower's claims have since been verified by statements from Rudy Giuliani and by testimony from members of President Trump's administration before Congress. And even President Trump has been unable to successfully deny any of the specific accusations in the complaint.

This isn't like a police officer writing you a ticket for drunk driving based on secondhand information. It's like being arrested based on the number you blew into a Breathalyzer, the open containers in your car, and your own admission that you were in fact under the influence.

If you're curious as to the specific evidence confirming the whistleblower's complaint, you don't have to take my word for it. The appendix at the end of this book contains not only the whistleblower's complaint but also the memo of President Trump's call with Zelensky, as well as the text messages exchanged among top US envoys pursuing Trump's quid pro quo. Of course, beyond these written materials, we've also seen President Trump defend his actions and invite foreign interference in the 2020 election in public — so we don't exactly need more evidence proving the veracity of the whistleblower's report.

Case Question #6: Did Hunter and Joe Biden break the law?

By all appearances, Vice President Biden and his son Hunter didn't break the law. Even Yuriy Lutsenko, the Ukrainian prosecutor who originally claimed that the Bidens were under investigation, has since retracted his accusation. "Hunter Biden did not violate any Ukrainian laws," he said in a May 2019 interview with *Bloomberg News.*

As to the accusation that Vice President Biden demanded that Ukraine fire a prosecutor who had been investigating Hunter Biden, Lutsenko said, "At the end of the day, Shokin submitted his own resignation." The investigation into Burisma, the company whose board Hunter Biden sat on, had been dormant by the time of Shokin's departure.

And as for US laws, neither the FBI nor the Department of Justice found any reason to charge either Hunter Biden or Vice President Biden.

But, of course, just because something's legal doesn't make it right.

Case Question #7: Is what Hunter Biden did wrong?

Absolutely. Hunter Biden had no real experience in the energy sector, which made him wholly unqualified to sit on the board of Burisma. The only logical reason the company could have had for appointing him was his ties to Vice President Biden. This kind of nepotism isn't only wrong; it is a potential danger to our country, since it makes it easier for foreign powers to buy influence.

The thing is: it's not illegal. That's why Hunter Biden didn't hide his involvement with Burisma. And it's why President Trump's children — Ivanka, Don Jr., and Eric — continue to conduct business around the world with impunity. As does President Trump's son-in-law, Jared Kushner, *who works in the White House.*

No politician, from either party, should allow a foreign power to conduct this kind of influence peddling with their family members.

End of story.

Case Question #8: Isn't President Trump allowed to fight corruption?

Of course. But as I discussed in Chapter 2, that's not what was happening here.

As Senator Romney tweeted, "When the only American citizen President Trump singles out . . . is his political opponent in the midst of the Democratic nomination process, it strains credulity to suggest that it is anything other than politically motivated." This is especially true because:

- When Trump was asked if he'd ever asked a foreign leader to launch a corruption investigation into someone who was not his political opponent, he couldn't name a single case;
- A member of President Trump's own administration wrote a formal letter to Congress saying Ukraine had been effectively combating corruption, with the express purpose of convincing Congress to send them aid. So it doesn't make much sense that President Trump would then do a blatant

about-face and object to doling out that aid on the basis of corruption;

- President Trump did not mention general corruption during his phone call with President Zelensky. Instead, he focused entirely on matters that would help his campaign;
- President Trump cut the State Department's budget for fighting corruption, which wouldn't make a whole lot of sense if that was genuinely one of his priorities. Indeed, he involved his private attorney, Rudy Giuliani, in all sorts of suspicious interactions instead of letting the State Department handle them;
- If President Trump really wanted to combat corruption in Ukraine, he would never have asked President Zelensky to go on television to announce an investigation. Serious law enforcement investigations are done in secret. What Trump wanted would have been a show investigation, designed not to find the truth but to damage Vice President Biden's reputation. If Trump really cared about fighting corruption, why did he want the investigation publicly announced? It strains credulity to think that this was about corruption, which is presumably why President Trump trotted out a grab bag of other defenses.

Case Question #9: Aren't the people voting on impeachment biased?

Yes. Everyone deciding whether or not President Trump should be impeached has a political bias — and many have expressed an opinion of his conduct on the record. This is, of course, very different from how a traditional jury is selected. As law professor

Charles Black writes: "In an ordinary judicial trial, persons in such a position would of course be disqualified to act, whether as judges or jurors." But, he notes, "it cannot have been the intention of the Framers that this rule apply in impeachments," since they wrote the Constitution in such a way that impeachment would be decided by politicians, who are biased by dint of their very positions.

"The remedy," he concludes, "has to be in the conscience of each senator, who ought to realize the danger and try as far as possible to divest himself of all prejudice." Black's point is what I've called the Yardstick Rule in this book — the idea that senators must apply a consistent yardstick in determining whether a given offense is impeachable, regardless of the president's political party.

Thankfully, this investigation is being led by Speaker Pelosi, who has exercised special caution in this case — as she has throughout her career. When many in her party sought to impeach President Trump over the Mueller report, she declined to do so. And back when Democrats were trying to impeach President Bush in 2008 over the Iraq war, she sided against them. She even went across the country on what the *New York Times* described as "the Why-Haven't-You-Impeached-the-President Tour." Across the board, Speaker Pelosi has viewed impeachment as a last resort.

Throughout our history, at moments of great consequence, partisans have been able to put aside their personal views for the good of the country. Just think about Senator Ross during President Johnson's impeachment. Or think about my frequent collaborator, George Conway, a lifelong conservative, married to one of President Trump's most important advisers, who has come forward time and again to document and describe the existential threat Trump's actions pose to our democracy. He's not the only public figure to break from his party. And it's my fervent hope that there will be more.

Case Question #10: Doesn't every politician ask for help from foreign powers? Why is foreign interference so bad anyway? Why is accepting it a high crime?

No, American politicians don't simply go around asking foreign powers to help them win elections. In fact, as I mentioned in Chapter 2, when President Trump's phone call with President Zelensky started to raise questions, the *New York Times* called up 10 former White House chiefs of staff, who worked under Obama, Bush Jr., Clinton, Bush Sr., and Reagan. They asked each of them whether they would have ever even considered working with a foreign power to win an election. Every single one of these chiefs of staff provided a definitive no.

Opposition to foreign interference in our elections is as old as America itself. In the opening pages of this book, I mentioned Washington's belief that "foreign influence is one of the most baneful foes of republican government," Adams's fear that "the danger of foreign influence" would "recur" as "often as elections happen," and Madison's belief that we needed impeachment in our Constitution to ensure that no president would "betray his trust to foreign powers."

In *Federalist No. 68*, Alexander Hamilton stated his view that the "most deadly adversaries of republican government" would come "chiefly from the desire in foreign powers to gain an improper ascendant in our councils."

"How could they better gratify this," he added, "than by raising a creature of their own to the chief magistracy of the Union?"

The reason our founders feared foreign interference was that they knew it had the power to undermine our democracy. Instead of the government reflecting the will of the American people, they worried, it could come to represent the interests of whichever foreign power intervened in a given election. (And, they recognized, foreign interference would be particularly pernicious if it were done in secret, as the Ukraine plot was supposed to be, because the American people would never know they were living under foreign influence — like puppets unaware of their puppet master.)

That's why our Constitution has so many protections designed to shield us from foreign influence, from the natural-born citizen clause, which states that "no Person except a natural born Citizen ... shall be eligible to the Office of President," to the emoluments clause, which states that "no Person holding any Office of Profit or Trust under them ... shall ... accept of any present, Emolument, Office, or Title, of any kind whatever, from any King, Prince, or foreign State."

And, of course, fear of foreign interference is also one of the reasons our Constitution granted Congress the power to impeach a president. As one of our founders, Edmund Randolph, told the Virginia Ratifying Convention, a president "may be impeached" for "receiving emoluments from foreign powers."

On October 21, 2019, President Trump called this clause in our Constitution, there since 1787, "phony."

Case Question #11: Is there actually any hope of 67 senators really voting to impeach President Trump?

Before Republicans decided to impeach President Nixon, they were vehemently opposed to the idea of impeaching him. Lawrence Hogan, the first Republican in Congress to announce his support for impeachment, didn't do so until right before the House Judiciary Committee was set to vote — only two weeks before President Nixon resigned. This stuff moves fast.

Until its final hours, the investigation into Watergate had been highly unpopular with the American public. Even after the Saturday Night Massacre, only 38 percent of Americans supported removing President Nixon from office. But as more citizens began to understand how he had abused his power, public support for impeachment began to increase — and, in turn, so did support for impeachment among Republicans in Congress.

While public support for impeachment never topped 57 percent, Republican senator Barry Goldwater — alongside House Republican leader John Jacob Rhodes and Senate Republican leader Hugh Scott — eventually paid a visit to the White House and told President Nixon that he had no choice but to resign. They did so despite the fact that over 50 percent of Republicans approved of his performance at the time.

This story by no means guarantees that President Trump will meet the same fate, but it is proof that sometimes Congress really does put country before party.

There are, after all, at least some similarities between President Nixon's impeachment and President Trump's. Lawrence Hogan, for instance, had a son, who, naturally, he named Larry. Now the governor of Maryland, Larry Hogan, a Republican, has channeled his father's courage and called for impeachment proceedings against Trump.

Perhaps Congress will follow the lead of a Lawrence Hogan once again.

One More Question

I could have answered hundreds of additional questions about the case against President Trump — from whether tweets are admissible in court as a form of witness intimidation (yes) to why President Trump hired Rudy Giuliani in the first place (who knows?). As I mentioned at the beginning of the chapter, I am happy to answer any of these questions if you send them to @neal_katyal.

But I kept this chapter concise because there's no need to over-complicate an open-and-shut case. You know what our Constitution says about impeachment. You know why President Trump's abuses of trust qualify as high crimes. And now you know how Congress can act to remove him.

Before I conclude this book, though, there's one more question I still have to address — a question whose answer may well be more important to the future of our country than anything else I've discussed:

> *What will become of our country if we impeach President Trump?*

That is the subject of the next, and final, chapter.

5

OUT OF MANY, ONE

*Try to impeach him. Just try it. You will have a spasm of
violence in this country, an insurrection, like you've never
seen. Both sides are heavily armed, my friend. This is not
1974. The people will not stand for impeachment. A politician who votes for it would be endangering their own life.*

Roger Stone, President Trump's longtime adviser, claims he
wasn't "advocating" violence when he said this to a reporter, he
was just "predicting" it.

On September 29, 2019, President Trump made a similar claim
on his Twitter page. "If the Democrats are successful in removing
the President from office," he wrote, quoting a Fox News guest, "it
will cause a Civil War like fracture in this Nation from which our
Country will never heal." This, Trump might argue, was a premo-
nition as well. He didn't intend to incite a "Civil War like fracture
in this Nation." He simply predicted one.

Trump's supporters, however, treated his words like a com-
mand. As my Georgetown colleague Mary McCord detailed in
Lawfare, a national security blog run by law professors, militias
around the country believed President Trump was calling them

to action with his tweet. Oath Keepers, a far-right armed organization, told its 24,000 followers that Trump's tweet brought our country to "the verge of a HOT civil war."

"This is the truth," its members wrote. "We ARE on the verge of a HOT civil war. Like in 1859. That's where we are. And the Right has ZERO trust or respect for anything the left is doing. We see THEM as illegitimate too."

This wasn't necessarily an empty threat. According to its website, Oath Keepers has trained Americans "in as many states as possible" to "serve as the local militia" if they are "called upon by President Trump to serve the nation." And, by all appearances, they own the guns to do it.

But we don't even need another Civil War for President Trump's impeachment to split our country at its seams. As Jelani Cobb wrote in *The New Yorker,* "The dark portent is not that Trump will inspire a reenactment of the central conflicts of America's past. It's that he will author a novel catastrophe all his own."

"Only When It Is Dark Enough"

This doesn't have to be our fate.

Yes, we are living through one of the darkest moments in the history of our country—and President Trump's impeachment could very well tear our country apart. Trump's voters could be left feeling that their voices have been shut out of our democracy. Trump's opponents could be left wondering if they will be the subjects of violence. Our house could be divided until it can no longer stand.

Or impeachment could bring out the best of America. As Martin Luther King, Jr., said in Memphis, Tennessee, on the eve of his assassination, "Only when it is dark enough can you see the stars." And despite everything we face, I believe we can get there.

Because I believe America is better than this moment. I believe our sense of weary resignation can be replaced with one of boundless resolve, and that while it's certain to be contentious, impeachment can serve as a fresh start for our nation. And I believe we are ready to move past the division, the violence, and the toxicity in our politics — so we can get back to work building a union that's a little more perfect tomorrow than it is today.

But we can only realize this dream if all of us — Democrats and Republicans and Americans who couldn't care less about politics — come together not only to protect our country from the kind of devastation Stone and Trump have envisaged taking place if President Trump is impeached, but also to strengthen our institutions so our democracy is never vulnerable to an attack like this again.

And the key to getting there is understanding that this impeachment is not about politics.

That's what makes the Ukraine case different from past inquiries — like the Starr report. This is one where Democrats can honestly say, without a shadow of a doubt, that they would have impeached a president of their own party for this behavior. And Republicans know in their hearts that they would have impeached a Democrat for an abuse of power like this a long time ago as well. The Yardstick Rule, in other words, leads Democrats and Republicans alike to the same verdict: guilty.

In the preceding pages I have explained why our laws and our history, from 1787 to the present day, have left Congress with no other choice, given what President Trump has already admitted doing and what he says he wants to do again. And I fervently believe that the House, and then the Senate, will do the right thing.

But then what? What comes next? If we impeach President

Trump, what reforms can we implement to try to prevent this from happening again?

The reality is President Trump has ignored regulations and laws since he first descended the escalator at Trump Tower, so I cannot promise that he would have behaved any differently if the laws had been different. But I can guarantee that the following policies would have made it easier to hold him accountable for his misdeeds. And while this is far from a comprehensive list, I hope it's a helpful start.

Reform #1: Campaign Finance

When officials at the Department of Justice were asked why they didn't investigate President Trump's phone call with President Zelensky after receiving the whistleblower's report, they blamed campaign finance laws — which state that a contribution from a foreign power is illegal only if it's a "thing of value." And because they couldn't place a direct value on the Ukrainian help, the DOJ tried to quietly close the investigation, hoping no one would find out about it.

Let's assume the DOJ's decision was in fact based on campaign finance laws rather than on a self-serving directive from President Trump or Attorney General Barr. Even then, the decision would have made no sense, because under existing law, accepting or soliciting any foreign contribution to a campaign with a value of $2,000 or more is considered a misdemeanor — while accepting any foreign contribution with a value of at least $25,000 is considered a felony. And clearly, an investigation into your political rival by a foreign government is worth *far more* than $2,000, or $25,000, to a campaign. After all, campaigns spend millions of dollars on negative advertisements, which could never be even nearly as effective as a publicly announced investigation by a foreign power.

What's more, our Federal Election Commission is already on the record saying that donations don't have to come in the form of cash for them to count as "things of value." As its chairman, Ellen Weintraub, wrote two days after the impeachment inquiry was opened: "The Commission has recognized the 'broad scope' of the foreign national contribution prohibition and found that even when the value of a good or service 'may be nominal or difficult to ascertain,' such contributions are nevertheless banned." In other words, just because President Trump didn't ask Ukraine to write him a check, under FEC guidelines he was still requesting that President Zelensky provide him with a "thing of value."

Elaborating on this point, Weintraub later said, "The law is pretty clear: it's absolutely illegal for anyone to solicit, accept, or receive anything of value from a foreign national in connection with any election in the United States."

"Solicit," of course, being the key word.

The president's lawyer Jay Sekulow, on the other hand, went on TV to claim that Special Counsel Mueller had found that foreign campaign help wasn't a "thing of value." When I heard him say that, I found it bizarre, as I didn't recall reading that in the Mueller report. Turns out, Mueller said the opposite. "Candidate-related opposition research given to a campaign for the purpose of influencing an election could constitute a contribution to which the foreign-source ban could apply," Mueller wrote. And that makes sense, as up until President Trump was elected, the Justice Department ruled that all sorts of things — even sexual relationships — count as "things of value."

This is all to say that President Trump's request to President

Zelensky was a clear campaign finance violation under existing laws — but to prevent the DOJ from making a similar ruling in the future, Congress should more clearly define a "thing of value" to include *any and all* coordination with a foreign power. We shouldn't really need this, in the sense that this is already what current law requires. But in the wake of the absurd DOJ position that help from Ukraine wasn't a "thing of value" because it could not be quantified (and also in the wake of Mueller grappling with the complexities of this issue in his final report), Congress needs to step in and clarify that a "thing of value" does *not* need to be quantifiable at a specific monetary value. That way, if a future candidate less blatantly (but still dangerously) solicits assistance from a foreign power, they can still be held accountable.

Reform #2: Tax Returns

This one is simple. All presidents and presidential candidates should have to release their tax returns well in advance of an election, because the public has a right to know whether their commander in chief is in debt to a foreign power.

Congress should pass a law requiring it.

Reform #3: The Special Counsel Regulations

Special Counsel Mueller's investigation is only indirectly related to the Ukraine inquiry, and as I explain in Chapters 3 and 4, I do not believe Congress should focus its case on Mueller's findings. Even if Trump and his campaign had no dealings with Russia in

2016, I would absolutely still advocate for President Trump being removed from office, solely on the basis of his conduct as president with respect to Ukraine.

That said, Mueller's investigation looms large over these impeachment proceedings, because some Americans have been led by Trump to believe that Mueller conducted a witch hunt, and as a result, they are disinclined to believe the findings of *any* investigation into the president's conduct. A large part of the skepticism borne in the wake of Mueller's report can be traced to the highly misleading and inaccurate summary of the report provided by Attorney General Barr, who didn't let the public see the full report for many weeks.

Shockingly, Barr's summary omitted Mueller's most important point: that his decision on whether to charge or exonerate President Trump for his 10 instances of obstruction of justice rested not on whether President Trump actually did in fact obstruct justice but on the DOJ memos arguing that a sitting president cannot be criminally indicted. In other words, Mueller didn't intend to clear President Trump of all wrongdoing. He simply meant to leave the decision of whether to charge him up to Congress — a point Attorney General Barr never communicated to the American people.

Part of the blame here, of course, rests with Mueller. By failing to speak up when Attorney General Barr distorted the findings of his report, he prevented the American people from learning that Barr's summary was misleading until public opinion had already been formed and skepticism about investigations into the president (like the Ukraine probe) had already been solidified. And while Special Counsel Mueller did express concerns to the attorney general in private, the public didn't find out about it until it was too late.

That's why we need to rewrite the special counsel regulations, so what happened with Mueller's report can never happen again.

In 1998 and 1999, as a young Justice Department lawyer during the Ken Starr investigations, I had the privilege of drafting the regulations that replaced the Independent Counsel Act (which gave Ken Starr his power) and have been used to govern the special counsel investigations that have taken place since — including the Mueller investigation. By and large, I believe these regulations have been effective, insofar as they've put in place a clear procedure by which the executive branch can conduct an unbiased investigation into the president of the United States (or another high-ranking public official). They've provided accountability and transparency into what would otherwise be closed and buried investigations; and the regulations are the reason the DOJ was forced to share the results of the Mueller investigation with Congress, including with the minority party. The Mueller probe wasn't toothless because of the special counsel regulations, but because of the DOJ opinions that prevented the Department of Justice from indicting a sitting president.

In a few pages I'll explain why I believe these DOJ opinions need to be reviewed — and partially reversed. But there are other steps we can take to build even more transparency into special counsel investigations.

The central challenge we face is ensuring that the public has access to the findings of the special counsel's report without its first being filtered by a presidential appointee like the attorney general of the United States. This is one of the oldest questions in government and can be traced back at least to the Roman poet and satirist Juvenal: *Quis custodiet ipsos custodes?* Who will guard the guards?

How, in other words, can we ensure that the executive branch can investigate itself without fear of intervention — direct or vicarious — from the president? Especially since Article II of the Constitution specifically puts the executive branch in charge of all federal investigations, meaning the process can't be outsourced to or controlled by Congress?

The answer lies in writing specific special counsel regulations for investigations of the commander in chief, mandating release of the full (unclassified) report to Congress before the attorney general can provide his spin in the form of a summary. This would ensure that coverage is based on the content of the report itself rather than on the self-serving "summary" by the president's appointees.

And even before the report is turned in, the regulations should require that if the attorney general were to interfere in any way with a special counsel's investigation, the report would be sent immediately and directly to the House and Senate Judiciary Committees. A special select committee of trusted committee members could then be used to hear such information in sensitive cases (perhaps the Republicans could pick three Democrats, and vice versa). The logistics can be determined later, but Trump's DOJ showed why we can't allow decisions surrounding special counsel reports to be made solely by appointees of the president without some kind of possibility for independent review.

We also certainly shouldn't allow the president to dodge being interviewed during special counsel investigations altogether, as President Trump did. This is why the Department of Justice should implement a regulation mandating that if the president refuses to speak to a special counsel investigating him, he will trigger a referral to Congress, where all options, including impeachment, will be on the table. This will help ensure that the president has an incentive to cooperate.

Reform #4: Indictment

As I've discussed, the Justice Department has two memos that say a sitting president cannot be indicted. But where does that leave us? As Walter Dellinger, another former acting solicitor general, once asked, "What does the nation do if it turns out that a president of the United States has committed serious crimes that a prosecutor can prove beyond a reasonable doubt?" Dellinger's answer was horrifying. "One possible resolution," he said, "would be to offer a plea bargain in which the commander in chief agreed to resign the presidency in exchange for utmost leniency. Perversely, the more financially corrupt or psychologically unstable the White House occupant, the greater his or her bargaining power: Only if you let my client go scot-free, a president's lawyers could argue, will you be allowed to pry the nuclear codes from his hands."

One of the reasons presidents have so much leverage is the statute of limitations, which states that someone can be convicted of a crime only if charges are brought within a certain window of the offense being committed. All Americans have this legal defense, but presidents have a unique ability to take advantage of it because they are barred from being prosecuted while in office, so by the time they leave, the statute of limitations on their conduct has often already expired. This means that instead of being inclined to resign, corrupt presidents have a warped incentive to stay in office for as long as possible. That doesn't make any sense.

We want presidents to run for reelection to help the country, not to help themselves.

There's a clear solution to this challenge — one that maintains much of the rationale for why a sitting president cannot be indicted — and it revolves around Dellinger's distinction between the two big phases of the criminal process: *indictment* and *trial.* There are lots of good reasons, as the Justice Department memos outline, that a sitting president cannot be forced to stand trial while in office. As Dellinger notes, the distraction could be overwhelming; and in general we want our presidents to focus on doing the nation's work. But what about *indictment*? Why can't a president even be formally accused?

Turns out the Justice Department memos don't really offer an answer; instead they lump accusation and trial together into one ball of wax. But these are two fundamentally different processes, and the DOJ could rewrite its rules to allow a president to be indicted even if he couldn't be tried. This small change would make a big difference, because it would extend the statute of limitations on the president's crimes, and it would also empower a future special counsel to take steps to indict instead of risking what happened to Mueller, when the president's defenders spun the report as a nothingburger.

I'm heartened by the fact that not only does Clinton's acting solicitor general, Walter Dellinger, believe we should allow the DOJ to indict the president, but so too does President George W. Bush's solicitor general, Ted Olson, who is a fervent believer in executive power. This should provide all of us with hope that after Trump's presidency we can find a bipartisan consensus around the idea that no one should be above the law — including the president of the United States.

Reform #5: Recusal Rules

When Attorney General Jeff Sessions recused himself from the Russia investigation, President Trump threatened to fire him and asked him to "unrecuse" himself. But as a subject of the investigation, Sessions had a moral and professional obligation to step aside. That's what every Justice Department official I know, from Republican and Democratic administrations, has always done — followed the advice of career ethics professionals and recused themselves if they were worried about a conflict of interest. That is, every Justice Department official until Attorney General Barr.

Since being appointed attorney general, William Barr has repeatedly refused to step aside from investigations that directly relate to him. This includes the Mueller probe, about which Barr sent President Trump a memo before becoming attorney general; and it includes the Ukraine investigation, in which he is directly implicated by both the whistleblower complaint and the "transcript." In fact, his Justice Department went as far as to suppress the complaint on the basis of a dubious reading of the campaign finance law, with Attorney General Barr in charge.

This is a clear case of the fox guarding the henhouse, which is why one of the leading bar associations in the nation, the New York City Bar Association, took the extraordinary step of criticizing Barr for not recusing, saying that "he should resign or, failing that, be subject to sanctions, including possible removal, by Congress."

There is a better way. The Justice Department already has a protocol for circumstances like these, in which Justice Management Division ethicists are supposed to make a recommendation on whether DOJ officials should recuse themselves from a case. The problem is that these decisions appear to have been ignored repeatedly over the course of the Trump presidency.

In the future, if the advice of the Justice Management Division ethicists is disregarded by an official in the DOJ, their decision should trigger a report to the House and Senate Judiciary Committee chair and ranking member (who is of the minority party). That report can be kept secret, of course, but there must be an opportunity for both political parties to be told of a grave and unusual situation in which a Justice Department official is participating in a matter over the objections of DOJ ethicists.

Reform #6: End White House Interference in Criminal Prosecutions

When I was a 28-year-old at the Justice Department, one of my first assignments was to think through the relationship between the White House and the DOJ. It's a fraught one. The Justice Department's leadership is appointed by the president, but at the same time, the DOJ is made up of lawyers who are supposed to be committed to justice, regardless of what the occupant of the White House may want.

For a long time, the White House and the DOJ have had a protocol in terms of communication about criminal cases. Some of the details vary a bit from one administration to the next, but the basic idea is the president should interfere with DOJ investigations as infrequently as possible. This is done both to ensure that criminal prosecutions aren't driven by politics and to avoid giving defendants an argument that they were selectively targeted and that their rights were violated by politicizing the criminal process.

Indeed, I know firsthand that during the Obama Administration, the idea of the president mentioning anything about a criminal prosecution was virtually verboten, and I very much suspect that this was the protocol in prior Republican administrations as well.

To be sure, there are times when the president or his close advisers need to be informed about criminal matters. If, for instance, the DOJ were going to levy charges against a foreign diplomat for being a spy and risk a major diplomatic rupture, or if the DOJ were going to prosecute a major company and throw our economy into a spiral, the president of the United States should of course know about that in advance. That way, the president can prepare for the diplomatic rupture or financial catastrophe that might result from the DOJ's decision.

But President Trump has revealed the dangers of keeping the president abreast of the DOJ's every move. He has thoroughly politicized law enforcement operations in a way that used to be a hypothetical in my law school classroom but is now our reality.

The risk here is the destruction of the rule of law, because if a president can open and shut DOJ investigations at will, letting his friends go and pursuing his enemies with the awesome force of a federal prosecution, then the DOJ will become a political tool instead of a law enforcement agency. And we know that President Trump is willing to do this, as his few acts of clemency have included political allies like Sheriff Joe Arpaio and Dinesh D'Souza. But at least pardons are done openly, since the president can't secretly pardon folks. By contrast, he *can* order the DOJ to quietly drop an investigation — as the DOJ decided to do with its inquiry into the whistleblower's complaint. (Whether or not President Trump was involved in that decision is not yet known.)

So what to do? I don't think it is realistic to bar the president from getting information about ongoing criminal investigations.

If Congress passed such a law, it would be unconstitutional, because Article II of the Constitution vests the prosecution power in the executive branch and this would be viewed as an interference with it, at least by the current Supreme Court. And if the president voluntarily bound himself to a policy to bar giving himself such information, it could risk hurting our government, too, because as I've said, sometimes the president does need to know about an impending criminal prosecution.

Here we can take a lesson from the regulations governing special counsel investigations. If the president ever interferes with a criminal investigation, his doing so should trigger an immediate reporting requirement to the chairman and ranking member of the House and Senate Judiciary Committees. Obviously such a scheme has risks, since Congress, a political body, generally shouldn't have a role in criminal investigations. But those risks are likely eclipsed by the risk of giving future presidents the untrammeled and politicized prosecution power that Trump has employed during his time in office.

Reform #7: Congressional Investigations

Right now, only members of the majority party in the House of Representatives can launch investigations. To understand the significance of this, one only needs to picture what would have happened if Democrats had not won the House in 2018. We likely would never have found out about the whistleblower's report or what Trump did to pressure Ukraine for personal and political gain.

Our ability to hold a president accountable should not depend on the composition of Congress, because if a Democratic president abuses his power, Republicans should be able to investigate his conduct even if they don't have 218 seats in the House. And vice versa. That's why Congress should revise its rules to allow investigations to be launched by the party that's in the minority as well as the one that's in the majority.

Mere Parchment

These legislative and regulatory changes would all make a difference — but in our democracy, the only reliable check we have on our president is the people. Our founders understood that. In *Federalist No. 48*, James Madison, who perhaps more than anyone else is responsible for our Constitution, wrote that our laws are mere "parchment barriers."

Our Constitution was designed to hold a president like Donald Trump accountable. He has wielded the powers of the presidency for the benefit of himself instead of for the benefit of the American people. He has undermined the integrity of our elections — and, in the process, jeopardized our national security by leaving us vulnerable to blackmail. He has obstructed justice into the investigations of his conduct, adopting an unconstitutional view of executive power. And he has promised to do it all again. Indeed, he *is* doing it all again.

These are the very high crimes our founders imagined when they decided to include impeachment in the Constitution. But President Trump will not be impeached by Article I, Section 4; or by Article 1, Section 3; or by Article 1, Section 9. Those words are mere parchment. President Trump will be impeached by human beings — members of Congress who are no different from you and me; who are as frightened of their decision as Barbara

Jordan and Walter Flowers and Paul Sarbanes were when they voted to remove President Nixon; who want to do what is best for our country but might not know how.

Members of Congress are human beings — as brave, as flawed, as brilliant, and as limited as each and every one of us — who will not find the right answer on their own. They need you to fill them with the courage they need to get there. So call your representatives, show up at their offices, and demand that they fulfill their constitutional duty. But don't stop there. Ask your neighbors to come with you; hand them your copy of this book; tell them why our democracy is counting on their leadership. Call your family members, even if their thoughts on politics make your turkey taste a little worse every Thanksgiving. *Especially* if they do. Listen to them — really listen to them — so you can understand where they're coming from, and then explain to them why you disagree.

This isn't about impeaching a president. This is about coming together around our shared belief that no one is above the law — and making sure we are never vulnerable to this kind of division again. This is about not only holding out America's motto as a goal to which we aspire but working every day to make it a reality.

E pluribus unum.

Out of many, one.

Acknowledgments

When people ask us how two people wrote a book in a handful of weeks, our answer is we didn't. Sure, two names — Neal and Sam — might be on the cover, but this book wouldn't have come together without countless others dropping everything to make this possible.

That starts with Howard Yoon, who believed in us, and believed in this project, before anyone else. Without him, this book wouldn't exist.

That's also true of Elena Vázquez and Jake Leffew, who woke up early in the morning and stayed up late at night to add serious heft to a book researched in a matter of weeks. The speed, the comprehensiveness, the diligence of their work was invaluable. And Julie Tate built on their contributions to ensure that we didn't publish any fake news.

Neal would also like to thank his management team at Friends at Work, and especially the unparalleled Ty Stiklorius, Lindsay Scola, and Andrea Sumpter.

Perhaps more than anyone else, we also owe our gratitude to Houghton Mifflin Harcourt — Alexander, Bruce, Olivia, Megan, Lori, and everyone else on the team, who edited, designed, and printed this book in record speed. Most publishers would have said we were crazy. (Some, of course, actually did.) But Houghton Mifflin Harcourt took a chance on this crazy project and then somehow made it happen.

We also couldn't conclude this acknowledgments section without thanking everyone who read this manuscript on such short notice, as well as our families, who are our whole world.

Appendix

This appendix includes several of the documents that are core to the case against President Trump. They include the whistleblower complaint, the White House summary of Trump's call with President Zelensky of Ukraine, the texts Ambassador Volker divulged, and the letter President Trump's lawyer sent to Congress, claiming unprecedented executive power.

For digital access to these documents, you can head over to www.nealkatyal.com. And as more evidence is published, we will be sure to include it there as well.

THE WHISTLEBLOWER COMPLAINT

August 12, 2019

The Honorable Richard Burr
Chairman
Select Committee on Intelligence
United States Senate

The Honorable Adam Schiff
Chairman
Permanent Select Committee on Intelligence
United States House of Representatives

Dear Chairman Burr and Chairman Schiff:

I am reporting an "urgent concern" in accordance with the procedures outlined in 50 U.S.C. §3033(k)(5)(A). This letter is UNCLASSIFIED when separated from the attachment.

In the course of my official duties, I have received information from multiple U.S. Government officials that the President of the United States is using the power of his office to solicit interference from a foreign country in the 2020 U.S. election. This interference includes, among other things, pressuring a foreign country to investigate one of the President's main domestic political rivals. The President's personal lawyer, Mr. Rudolph Giuliani, is a central figure in this effort. Attorney General Barr appears to be involved as well.

- Over the past four months, more than half a dozen U.S. officials have informed me of various facts related to this effort. The information provided herein was relayed to me in the course of official interagency business. It is routine for U.S. officials with responsibility for a particular regional or functional portfolio to share such information with one another in order to inform policymaking and analysis.
- I was not a direct witness to most of the events described. However, I found my colleagues' accounts of these events to be credible because, in almost all cases, multiple officials recounted fact patterns that were consistent with one another. In addition, a variety of information consistent with these private accounts has been reported publicly.

I am deeply concerned that the actions described below constitute "a serious or flagrant problem, abuse, or violation of law or Executive Order" that "does not include differences of opinions concerning public policy matters," consistent with the definition of an "urgent concern" in 50 U.S.C. §3033(k)(5)(G). I am therefore fulfilling my duty to report this information, through proper legal channels, to the relevant authorities.

- I am also concerned that these actions pose risks to U.S. national security and undermine the U.S. Government's efforts to deter and counter foreign interference in U.S. elections.

UNCLASSIFIED

To the best of my knowledge, the entirety of this statement is unclassified when separated from the classified enclosure. I have endeavored to apply the classification standards outlined in Executive Order (EO) 13526 and to separate out information that I know or have reason to believe is classified for national security purposes.[1]

- If a classification marking is applied retroactively, I believe it is incumbent upon the classifying authority to explain why such a marking was applied, and to which specific information it pertains.

I. The 25 July Presidential phone call

Early in the morning of 25 July, the President spoke by telephone with Ukrainian President Volodymyr Zelenskyy. I do not know which side initiated the call. This was the first publicly acknowledged call between the two leaders since a brief congratulatory call after Mr. Zelenskyy won the presidency on 21 April.

Multiple White House officials with direct knowledge of the call informed me that, after an initial exchange of pleasantries, the President used the remainder of the call to advance his personal interests. Namely, he sought to pressure the Ukrainian leader to take actions to help the President's 2020 reelection bid. According to the White House officials who had direct knowledge of the call, the President pressured Mr. Zelenskyy to, inter alia:

- initiate or continue an investigation[2] into the activities of former Vice President Joseph Biden and his son, Hunter Biden;
- assist in purportedly uncovering that allegations of Russian interference in the 2016 U.S. presidential election originated in Ukraine, with a specific request that the Ukrainian leader locate and turn over servers used by the Democratic National Committee (DNC) and examined by the U.S. cyber security firm Crowdstrike,[3] which initially reported that Russian hackers had penetrated the DNC's networks in 2016; and
- meet or speak with two people the President named explicitly as his personal envoys on these matters, Mr. Giuliani and Attorney General Barr, to whom the President referred multiple times in tandem.

---

[1] Apart from the information in the Enclosure, it is my belief that none of the information contained herein meets the definition of "classified information" outlined in EO 13526, Part 1, Section 1.1. There is ample open-source information about the efforts I describe below, including statements by the President and Mr. Giuliani. In addition, based on my personal observations, there is discretion with respect to the classification of private comments by or instructions from the President, including his communications with foreign leaders; information that is not related to U.S. foreign policy or national security—such as the information contained in this document, when separated from the Enclosure—is generally treated as unclassified. I also believe that applying a classification marking to this information would violate EO 13526, Part 1, Section 1.7, which states: "In no case shall information be classified, continue to be maintained as classified, or fail to be declassified in order to: (1) conceal violations of law, inefficiency, or administrative error; [or] (2) prevent embarrassment to a person, organization, or agency."

[2] It is unclear whether such a Ukrainian investigation exists. See Footnote #7 for additional information.

[3] I do not know why the President associates these servers with Ukraine. (See, for example, his comments to *Fox News* on 20 July: "And Ukraine. Take a look at Ukraine. How come the FBI didn't take this server? Podesta told them to get out. He said, get out. So, how come the FBI didn't take the server from the DNC?")

UNCLASSIFIED

The President also praised Ukraine's Prosecutor General, Mr. Yuriy Lutsenko, and suggested that Mr. Zelenskyy might want to keep him in his position. (Note: Starting in March 2019, Mr. Lutsenko made a series of public allegations—many of which he later walked back—about the Biden family's activities in Ukraine, Ukrainian officials' purported involvement in the 2016 U.S. election, and the activities of the U.S. Embassy in Kyiv. See Part IV for additional context.)

The White House officials who told me this information were deeply disturbed by what had transpired in the phone call. They told me that there was already a "discussion ongoing" with White House lawyers about how to treat the call because of the likelihood, in the officials' retelling, that they had witnessed the President abuse his office for personal gain.

The Ukrainian side was the first to publicly acknowledge the phone call. On the evening of 25 July, a readout was posted on the website of the Ukrainian President that contained the following line (translation from original Russian-language readout):

- "Donald Trump expressed his conviction that the new Ukrainian government will be able to quickly improve Ukraine's image and complete the investigation of corruption cases that have held back cooperation between Ukraine and the United States."

Aside from the above-mentioned "cases" purportedly dealing with the Biden family and the 2016 U.S. election, I was told by White House officials that no other "cases" were discussed.

Based on my understanding, there were approximately a dozen White House officials who listened to the call—a mixture of policy officials and duty officers in the White House Situation Room, as is customary. The officials I spoke with told me that participation in the call had not been restricted in advance because everyone expected it would be a "routine" call with a foreign leader. I do not know whether anyone was physically present with the President during the call.

- In addition to White House personnel, I was told that a State Department official, Mr. T. Ulrich Brechbuhl, also listened in on the call.
- I was not the only non-White House official to receive a readout of the call. Based on my understanding, multiple State Department and Intelligence Community officials were also briefed on the contents of the call as outlined above.

II.   Efforts to restrict access to records related to the call

In the days following the phone call, I learned from multiple U.S. officials that senior White House officials had intervened to "lock down" all records of the phone call, especially the official word-for-word transcript of the call that was produced—as is customary—by the White House Situation Room. This set of actions underscored to me that White House officials understood the gravity of what had transpired in the call.

- White House officials told me that they were "directed" by White House lawyers to remove the electronic transcript from the computer system in which such transcripts are typically stored for coordination, finalization, and distribution to Cabinet-level officials.

- Instead, the transcript was loaded into a separate electronic system that is otherwise used to store and handle classified information of an especially sensitive nature. One White House official described this act as an abuse of this electronic system because the call did not contain anything remotely sensitive from a national security perspective.

I do not know whether similar measures were taken to restrict access to other records of the call, such as contemporaneous handwritten notes taken by those who listened in.

III. Ongoing concerns

On 26 July, a day after the call, U.S. Special Representative for Ukraine Negotiations Kurt Volker visited Kyiv and met with President Zelenskyy and a variety of Ukrainian political figures. Ambassador Volker was accompanied in his meetings by U.S. Ambassador to the European Union Gordon Sondland. Based on multiple readouts of these meetings recounted to me by various U.S. officials, Ambassadors Volker and Sondland reportedly provided advice to the Ukrainian leadership about how to "navigate" the demands that the President had made of Mr. Zelenskyy.

I also learned from multiple U.S. officials that, on or about 2 August, Mr. Giuliani reportedly traveled to Madrid to meet with one of President Zelenskyy's advisers, Andriy Yermak. The U.S. officials characterized this meeting, which was not reported publicly at the time, as a "direct follow-up" to the President's call with Mr. Zelenskyy about the "cases" they had discussed.

- Separately, multiple U.S. officials told me that Mr. Giuliani had reportedly privately reached out to a variety of other Zelenskyy advisers, including Chief of Staff Andriy Bohdan and Acting Chairman of the Security Service of Ukraine Ivan Bakanov.[4]
- I do not know whether those officials met or spoke with Mr. Giuliani, but I was told separately by multiple U.S. officials that Mr. Yermak and Mr. Bakanov intended to travel to Washington in mid-August.

On 9 August, the President told reporters: "I think [President Zelenskyy] is going to make a deal with President Putin, and he will be invited to the White House. And we look forward to seeing him. He's already been invited to the White House, and he wants to come. And I think he will. He's a very reasonable guy. He wants to see peace in Ukraine, and I think he will be coming very soon, actually."

IV. Circumstances leading up to the 25 July Presidential phone call

Beginning in late March 2019, a series of articles appeared in an online publication called *The Hill*. In these articles, several Ukrainian officials—most notably, Prosecutor General Yuriy Lutsenko—made a series of allegations against other Ukrainian officials and current and former U.S. officials. Mr. Lutsenko and his colleagues alleged, *inter alia*:

---

[4] In a report published by the Organized Crime and Corruption Reporting Project (OCCRP) on 22 July, two associates of Mr. Giuliani reportedly traveled to Kyiv in May 2019 and met with Mr. Bakanov and another close Zelenskyy adviser, Mr. Serhiy Shefir.

UNCLASSIFIED

- that they possessed evidence that Ukrainian officials—namely, Head of the National Anticorruption Bureau of Ukraine Artem Sytnyk and Member of Parliament Serhiy Leshchenko—had "interfered" in the 2016 U.S. presidential election, allegedly in collaboration with the DNC and the U.S. Embassy in Kyiv;[5]
- that the U.S. Embassy in Kyiv—specifically, U.S. Ambassador Marie Yovanovitch, who had criticized Mr. Lutsenko's organization for its poor record on fighting corruption—had allegedly obstructed Ukrainian law enforcement agencies' pursuit of corruption cases, including by providing a "do not prosecute" list, and had blocked Ukrainian prosecutors from traveling to the United States expressly to prevent them from delivering their "evidence" about the 2016 U.S. election;[6] and
- that former Vice President Biden had pressured former Ukrainian President Petro Poroshenko in 2016 to fire then Ukrainian Prosecutor General Viktor Shokin in order to quash a purported criminal probe into Burisma Holdings, a Ukrainian energy company on whose board the former Vice President's son, Hunter, sat.[7]

In several public comments,[8] Mr. Lutsenko also stated that he wished to communicate directly with Attorney General Barr on these matters.[9]

The allegations by Mr. Lutsenko came on the eve of the first round of Ukraine's presidential election on 31 March. By that time, Mr. Lutsenko's political patron, President Poroshenko, was trailing Mr. Zelenskyy in the polls and appeared likely to be defeated. Mr. Zelenskyy had made known his desire to replace Mr. Lutsenko as Prosecutor General. On 21 April, Mr. Poroshenko lost the runoff to Mr. Zelenskyy by a landslide. See Enclosure for additional information.

---

[5] Mr. Sytnyk and Mr. Leshchenko are two of Mr. Lutsenko's main domestic rivals. Mr. Lutsenko has no legal training and has been widely criticized in Ukraine for politicizing criminal probes and using his tenure as Prosecutor General to protect corrupt Ukrainian officials. He has publicly feuded with Mr. Sytnyk, who heads Ukraine's only competent anticorruption body, and with Mr. Leshchenko, a former investigative journalist who has repeatedly criticized Mr. Lutsenko's record. In December 2018, a Ukrainian court upheld a complaint by a Member of Parliament, Mr. Boryslav Rozenblat, who alleged that Mr. Sytnyk and Mr. Leshchenko had "interfered" in the 2016 U.S. election by publicizing a document detailing corrupt payments made by former Ukrainian President Viktor Yanukovych before his ouster in 2014. Mr. Rozenblat had originally filed the motion in late 2017 after attempting to flee Ukraine amid an investigation into his taking of a large bribe. On 16 July 2019, Mr. Leshchenko publicly stated that a Ukrainian court had overturned the lower court's decision.

[6] Mr. Lutsenko later told Ukrainian news outlet *The Babel* on 17 April that Ambassador Yovanovitch had never provided such a list, and that he was, in fact, the one who requested such a list.

[7] Mr. Lutsenko later told *Bloomberg* on 16 May that former Vice President Biden and his son were not subject to any current Ukrainian investigations, and that he had no evidence against them. Other senior Ukrainian officials also contested his original allegations; one former senior Ukrainian prosecutor told *Bloomberg* on 7 May that Mr. Shokin in fact was not investigating Burisma at the time of his removal in 2016.

[8] See, for example, Mr. Lutsenko's comments to *The Hill* on 1 and 7 April and his interview with *The Babel* on 17 April, in which he stated that he had spoken with Mr. Giuliani about arranging contact with Attorney General Barr.

[9] In May, Attorney General Barr announced that he was initiating a probe into the "origins" of the Russia investigation. According to the above-referenced OCCRP report (22 July), two associates of Mr. Giuliani claimed to be working with Ukrainian officials to uncover information that would become part of this inquiry. In an interview with *Fox News* on 8 August, Mr. Giuliani claimed that Mr. John Durham, whom Attorney General Barr designated to lead this probe, was "spending a lot of time in Europe" because he was "investigating Ukraine." I do not know the extent to which, if at all, Mr. Giuliani is directly coordinating his efforts on Ukraine with Attorney General Barr or Mr. Durham.

- It was also publicly reported that Mr. Giuliani had met on at least two occasions with Mr. Lutsenko: once in New York in late January and again in Warsaw in mid-February. In addition, it was publicly reported that Mr. Giuliani had spoken in late 2018 to former Prosecutor General Shokin, in a Skype call arranged by two associates of Mr. Giuliani.[10]
- On 25 April in an interview with *Fox News*, the President called Mr. Lutsenko's claims "big" and "incredible" and stated that the Attorney General "would want to see this."

On or about 29 April, I learned from U.S. officials with direct knowledge of the situation that Ambassador Yovanovitch had been suddenly recalled to Washington by senior State Department officials for "consultations" and would most likely be removed from her position.

- Around the same time, I also learned from a U.S. official that "associates" of Mr. Giuliani were trying to make contact with the incoming Zelenskyy team.[11]
- On 6 May, the State Department announced that Ambassador Yovanovitch would be ending her assignment in Kyiv "as planned."
- However, several U.S. officials told me that, in fact, her tour was curtailed because of pressure stemming from Mr. Lutsenko's allegations. Mr. Giuliani subsequently stated in an interview with a Ukrainian journalist published on 14 May that Ambassador Yovanovitch was "removed...because she was part of the efforts against the President."

On 9 May, *The New York Times* reported that Mr. Giuliani planned to travel to Ukraine to press the Ukrainian government to pursue investigations that would help the President in his 2020 reelection bid.

- In his multitude of public statements leading up to and in the wake of the publication of this article, Mr. Giuliani confirmed that he was focused on encouraging Ukrainian authorities to pursue investigations into alleged Ukrainian interference in the 2016 U.S. election and alleged wrongdoing by the Biden family.[12]
- On the afternoon of 10 May, the President stated in an interview with *Politico* that he planned to speak with Mr. Giuliani about the trip.
- A few hours later, Mr. Giuliani publicly canceled his trip, claiming that Mr. Zelenskyy was "surrounded by enemies of the [U.S.] President...and of the United States."

On 11 May, Mr. Lutsenko met for two hours with President-elect Zelenskyy, according to a public account given several days later by Mr. Lutsenko. Mr. Lutsenko publicly stated that he had told Mr. Zelenskyy that he wished to remain as Prosecutor General.

---

[10] See, for example, the above-referenced articles in *Bloomberg* (16 May) and OCCRP (22 July).

[11] I do not know whether these associates of Mr. Giuliani were the same individuals named in the 22 July report by OCCRP, referenced above.

[12] See, for example, Mr. Giuliani's appearance on *Fox News* on 6 April and his tweets on 23 April and 10 May. In his interview with *The New York Times*, Mr. Giuliani stated that the President "basically knows what I'm doing, sure, as his lawyer." Mr. Giuliani also stated: "We're not meddling in an election, we're meddling in an investigation, which we have a right to do... There's nothing illegal about it... Somebody could say it's improper. And this isn't foreign policy – I'm asking them to do an investigation that they're doing already and that other people are telling them to stop. And I'm going to give them reasons why they shouldn't stop it because that information will be very, very helpful to my client, and may turn out to be helpful to my government."

UNCLASSIFIED

Starting in mid-May, I heard from multiple U.S. officials that they were deeply concerned by what they viewed as Mr. Giuliani's circumvention of national security decisionmaking processes to engage with Ukrainian officials and relay messages back and forth between Kyiv and the President. These officials also told me:

- that State Department officials, including Ambassadors Volker and Sondland, had spoken with Mr. Giuliani in an attempt to "contain the damage" to U.S. national security; and
- that Ambassadors Volker and Sondland during this time period met with members of the new Ukrainian administration and, in addition to discussing policy matters, sought to help Ukrainian leaders understand and respond to the differing messages they were receiving from official U.S. channels on the one hand, and from Mr. Giuliani on the other.

During this same timeframe, multiple U.S. officials told me that the Ukrainian leadership was led to believe that a meeting or phone call between the President and President Zelenskyy would depend on whether Zelenskyy showed willingness to "play ball" on the issues that had been publicly aired by Mr. Lutsenko and Mr. Giuliani. (Note: This was the general understanding of the state of affairs as conveyed to me by U.S. officials from late May into early July. I do not know who delivered this message to the Ukrainian leadership, or when.) See Enclosure for additional information.

Shortly after President Zelenskyy's inauguration, it was publicly reported that Mr. Giuliani met with two other Ukrainian officials: Ukraine's Special Anticorruption Prosecutor, Mr. Nazar Kholodnytskyy, and a former Ukrainian diplomat named Andriy Telizhenko. Both Mr. Kholodnytskyy and Mr. Telizhenko are allies of Mr. Lutsenko and made similar allegations in the above-mentioned series of articles in *The Hill*.

On 13 June, the President told *ABC*'s George Stephanopoulos that he would accept damaging information on his political rivals from a foreign government.

On 21 June, Mr. Giuliani tweeted: "New Pres of Ukraine still silent on investigation of Ukrainian interference in 2016 and alleged Biden bribery of Poroshenko. Time for leadership and investigate both if you want to purge how Ukraine was abused by Hillary and Clinton people."

In mid-July, I learned of a sudden change of policy with respect to U.S. assistance for Ukraine. See Enclosure for additional information.

ENCLOSURE: Classified appendix

TOP SECRET/███████████

August 12, 2019

(U) CLASSIFIED APPENDIX

(U) Supplementary classified information is provided as follows:

(U) Additional information related to Section II

(TS/████) According to multiple White House officials I spoke with, the transcript of the President's call with President Zelenskyy was placed into a computer system managed directly by the National Security Council (NSC) Directorate for Intelligence Programs. This is a standalone computer system reserved for codeword-level intelligence information, such as covert action. According to information I received from White House officials, some officials voiced concerns internally that this would be an abuse of the system and was not consistent with the responsibilities of the Directorate for Intelligence Programs. According to White House officials I spoke with, this was "not the first time" under this Administration that a Presidential transcript was placed into this codeword-level system solely for the purpose of protecting politically sensitive—rather than national security sensitive—information.

(U) Additional information related to Section IV

(S/████) I would like to expand upon two issues mentioned in Section IV that might have a connection with the overall effort to pressure the Ukrainian leadership. As I do not know definitively whether the below-mentioned decisions are connected to the broader efforts I describe, I have chosen to include them in the classified annex. If they indeed represent genuine policy deliberations and decisions formulated to advance U.S. foreign policy and national security, one might be able to make a reasonable case that the facts are classified.

- (S/████) I learned from U.S. officials that, on or around 14 May, the President instructed Vice President Pence to cancel his planned travel to Ukraine to attend President

Zelenskyy's inauguration on 20 May; Secretary of Energy Rick Perry led the delegation instead. According to these officials, it was also "made clear" to them that the President did not want to meet with Mr. Zelenskyy until he saw how Zelenskyy "chose to act" in office. I do not know how this guidance was communicated, or by whom. I also do not know whether this action was connected with the broader understanding, described in the unclassified letter, that a meeting or phone call between the President and President Zelenskyy would depend on whether Zelenskyy showed willingness to "play ball" on the issues that had been publicly aired by Mr. Lutsenko and Mr. Giuliani.

- (S/██) On 18 July, an Office of Management and Budget (OMB) official informed Departments and Agencies that the President "earlier that month" had issued instructions to suspend all U.S. security assistance to Ukraine. Neither OMB nor the NSC staff knew why this instruction had been issued. During interagency meetings on 23 July and 26 July, OMB officials again stated explicitly that the instruction to suspend this assistance had come directly from the President, but they still were unaware of a policy rationale. As of early August, I heard from U.S. officials that some Ukrainian officials were aware that U.S. aid might be in jeopardy, but I do not know how or when they learned of it.

THE JULY 25 CALL SUMMARY

UNCLASSIFIED [PkgNumberShort]

EYES ONLY
DO NOT COPY

MEMORANDUM OF TELEPHONE CONVERSATION

SUBJECT: (C) Telephone Conversation with President
                Zelenskyy of Ukraine

PARTICIPANTS: President Zelenskyy of Ukraine

                Notetakers: The White House Situation Room

DATE, TIME   July 25, 2019, 9:03 - 9:33 a.m. EDT
AND PLACE: Residence

(S/NF) The President: Congratulations on a great victory. We all
watched from the United States and you did a terrific job. The
way you came from behind, somebody who wasn't given much of a
chance, and you ended up winning easily. It's a fantastic
achievement. Congratulations.

(S/NF) President Zelenskyy: You are absolutely right Mr.
President. We did win big and we worked hard for this. We worked
a lot but I would like to confess to you that I had an
opportunity to learn from you. We used quite a few of your
skills and knowledge and were able to use it as an example for
our elections and yes it is true that these were unique
elections. We were in a unique situation that we were able to

CAUTION: A Memorandum of a Telephone Conversation (TELCON) is not a verbatim transcript of a
discussion. The text in this document records the notes and recollections of Situation Room Duty
Officers and NSC policy staff assigned to listen and memorialize the conversation in written form
as the conversation takes place. A number of factors can affect the accuracy of the record,
including poor telecommunications connections and variations in accent and/or interpretation.
The word "inaudible" is used to indicate portions of a conversation that the notetaker was unable
to hear.

UNCLASSIFIED

2   **UNCLASSIFIED**

achieve a unique success. I'm able to tell you the following;
the first time, you called me to congratulate me when I won my
presidential election, and the second time you are now calling
me when my party won the parliamentary election. I think I
should run more often so you can call me more often and we can
talk over the phone more often.

(S/NF) The President: [laughter] That's a very good idea. I
think your country is very happy about that.

(S/NF) President Zelenskyy: Well yes, to tell you the truth, we
are trying to work hard because we wanted to drain the swamp
here in our country. We brought in many many new people. Not the
old politicians, not the typical politicians, because we want to
have a new format and a new type of government. You are a great
teacher for us and in that.

(S/NF) The President: Well it's very nice of you to say that. I
will say that we do a lot for Ukraine. We spend a lot of effort
and a lot of time. Much more than the European countries are
doing and they should be helping you more than they are. Germany
does almost nothing for you. All they do is talk and I think
it's something that you should really ask them about. When I was
speaking to Angela Merkel she talks Ukraine, but she doesn't do
anything. A lot of the European countries are the same way so I
think it's something you want to look at but the United States
has been very very good to Ukraine. I wouldn't say that it's
reciprocal necessarily because things are happening that are not
good but the United States has been very very good to Ukraine.

(S/NF) President Zelenskyy: Yes you are absolutely right. Not
only 100%, but actually 1000% and I can tell you the following;
I did talk to Angela Merkel and I did meet with her. I also met
and talked with Macron and I told them that they are not doing
quite as much as they need to be doing on the issues with the
sanctions. They are not enforcing the sanctions. They are not
working as much as they should work for Ukraine. It turns out
that even though logically, the European Union should be our
biggest partner but technically the United States is a much
bigger partner than the European Union and I'm very grateful to
you for that because the United States is doing quite a lot for
Ukraine. Much more than the European Union especially when we
are talking about sanctions against the Russian Federation. I
would also like to thank you for your great support in the area
of defense. We are ready to continue to cooperate for the next
steps specifically we are almost ready to buy more Javelins from
the United States for defense purposes.

UNCLASSIFIED

3 UNCLASSIFIED

The President: I would like you to do us a favor though because our country has been through a lot and Ukraine knows a lot about it. I would like you to find out what happened with this whole situation with Ukraine, they say Crowdstrike... I guess you have one of your wealthy people... The server, they say Ukraine has it. There are a lot of things that went on, the whole situation. I think you're surrounding yourself with some of the same people. I would like to have the Attorney General call you or your people and I would like you to get to the bottom of it. As you saw yesterday, that whole nonsense ended with a very poor performance by a man named Robert Mueller, an incompetent performance, but they say a lot of it started with Ukraine. Whatever you can do, it's very important that you do it if that's possible.

President Zelenskyy: Yes it is very important for me and everything that you just mentioned earlier. For me as a President, it is very important and we are open for any future cooperation. We are ready to open a new page on cooperation in relations between the United States and Ukraine. For that purpose, I just recalled our ambassador from United States and he will be replaced by a very competent and very experienced ambassador who will work hard on making sure that our two nations are getting closer. I would also like and hope to see him having your trust and your confidence and have personal relations with you so we can cooperate even more so. I will personally tell you that one of my assistants spoke with Mr. Giuliani just recently and we are hoping very much that Mr. Giuliani will be able to travel to Ukraine and we will meet once he comes to Ukraine. I just wanted to assure you once again that you have nobody but friends around us. I will make sure that I surround myself with the best and most experienced people. I also wanted to tell you that we are friends. We are great friends and you Mr. President have friends in our country so we can continue our strategic partnership. I also plan to surround myself with great people and in addition to that investigation, I guarantee as the President of Ukraine that all the investigations will be done openly and candidly. That I can assure you.

The President: Good because I heard you had a prosecutor who was very good and he was shut down and that's really unfair. A lot of people are talking about that, the way they shut your very good prosecutor down and you had some very bad people involved. Mr. Giuliani is a highly respected man. He was the mayor of New York City, a great mayor, and I would like him to

UNCLASSIFIED

call you. I will ask him to call you along with the Attorney General. Rudy very much knows what's happening and he is a very capable guy. If you could speak to him that would be great. The former ambassador from the United States, the woman, was bad news and the people she was dealing with in the Ukraine were bad news so I just want to let you know that. The other thing, There's a lot of talk about Biden's son, that Biden stopped the prosecution and a lot of people want to find out about that so whatever you can do with the Attorney General would be great. Biden went around bragging that he stopped the prosecution so if you can look into it… It sounds horrible to me.

(S/NF) President Zelenskyy: I wanted to tell you about the prosecutor. First of all I understand and I'm knowledgeable about the situation. Since we have won the absolute majority in our Parliament, the next prosecutor general will be 100% my person, my candidate, who will be approved by the parliament and will start as a new prosecutor in September. He or she will look into the situation, specifically to the company that you mentioned in this issue. The issue of the investigation of the case is actually the issue of making sure to restore the honesty so we will take care of that and will work on the investigation of the case. On top of that, I would kindly ask you if you have any additional information that you can provide to us, it would be very helpful for the investigation to make sure that we administer justice in our country with regard to the Ambassador to the United States from Ukraine as far as I recall her name was Ivanovich. It was great that you were the first one who told me that she was a bad ambassador because I agree with you 100%. Her attitude towards me was far from the best as she admired the previous President and she was on his side. She would not accept me as a new President well enough.

(S/NF) The President: Well, she's going to go through some things. I will have Mr. Giuliani give you a call and I am also going to have Attorney General Barr call and we will get to the bottom of it. I'm sure you will figure it out. I heard the prosecutor was treated very badly and he was a very fair prosecutor so good luck with everything. Your economy is going to get better and better I predict. You have a lot of assets. It's a great country. I have many Ukrainian friends, their incredible people.

(S/NF) President Zelenskyy: I would like to tell you that I also have quite a few Ukrainian friends that live in the United States. Actually last time I traveled to the United States, I stayed in New York near Central Park and I stayed at the Trump

5 **UNCLASSIFIED**

Tower. I will talk to them and I hope to see them again in the
future. I also wanted to thank you for your invitation to visit
the United States, specifically Washington DC. On the other
hand, I also want to ensure you that we will be very serious
about the case and will work on the investigation. As to the
economy, there is much potential for our two countries and one
of the issues that is very important for Ukraine is energy
independence. I believe we can be very successful and
cooperating on energy independence with United States. We are
already working on cooperation. We are buying American oil but I
am very hopeful for a future meeting. We will have more time and
more opportunities to discuss these opportunities and get to
know each other better. I would like to thank you very much for
your support

(S/NF) The President: Good. Well, thank you very much and I
appreciate that. I will tell Rudy and Attorney General Barr to
call. Thank you. Whenever you would like to come to the White
House, feel free to call. Give us a date and we'll work that
out. I look forward to seeing you.

(S/NF) President Zelenskyy: Thank you very much. I would be very
happy to come and would be happy to meet with you personally and
get to know you better. I am looking forward to our meeting and
I also would like to invite you to visit Ukraine and come to the
city of Kyiv which is a beautiful city. We have a beautiful
country which would welcome you. On the other hand, I believe
that on September 1 we will be in Poland and we can meet in
Poland hopefully. After that, it might be a very good idea for
you to travel to Ukraine. We can either take my plane and go to
Ukraine or we can take your plane, which is probably much better
than mine.

(S/NF) The President: Okay, we can work that out. I look forward
to seeing you in Washington and maybe in Poland because I think
we are going to be there at that time.

(S/NF) President Zelenskyy: Thank you very much Mr. President.

(S/NF) The President: Congratulations on a fantastic job you've
done. The whole world was watching. I'm not sure it was so much
of an upset but congratulations.

(S/NF) President Zelenskyy: Thank you Mr. President bye-bye.

-- End of Conversation --

UNCLASSIFIED

THE TEXT MESSAGES

October 3, 2019

Members of the Intelligence, Oversight and Reform, and Foreign Affairs Committees
Washington, D.C. 20515

Dear Colleagues:

We are writing to convey our grave concerns with the unprecedented actions of President Donald Trump and his Administration with respect to the House of Representatives' impeachment inquiry.

The President and his aides are engaging in a campaign of misinformation and misdirection in an attempt to normalize the act of soliciting foreign powers to interfere in our elections.

We have all now seen the summary of the call in which President Trump repeatedly urged the Ukrainian President to launch an investigation into former Vice President Joe Biden—immediately after the Ukrainian President mentioned critical U.S. military assistance to counter Russian aggression.

The President claims he did nothing wrong. Even more astonishing, he is now openly and publicly asking another foreign power—China—to launch its own sham investigation against the Bidens to further his own political aims.

This is not normal or acceptable. It is unethical, unpatriotic, and wrong. American Presidents should never press foreign powers to target their domestic political rivals. Engaging in these stunning abuses in broad daylight does not absolve President Trump of his wrongdoings—or his grave offenses against the Constitution.

Over the past week, new reports have revealed that other Trump Administration officials also may have been involved in the illicit effort to get Ukrainian help for the President's campaign.

For example, Secretary of State Mike Pompeo has now admitted that he was on the call when President Trump explicitly pressed the Ukrainian President to investigate the Bidens—but failed to report this to the FBI or other law enforcement authorities. You will recall, FBI Director Christopher Wray urged individuals to report efforts to seek or receive help from a foreign power that may intervene in a U.S. presidential election.

This obligation is not diminished when the instigator of that foreign intervention is the President of the United States; it is all the more crucial to the security of our elections. Instead, when asked by the media about his own knowledge or participation in the call, Secretary Pompeo dissembled.

Likewise, we are investigating reports that Vice President Mike Pence may have been made aware of the contents of the call, and his absence from the Ukrainian President's inauguration may have been related to efforts to put additional pressure on Ukraine to deliver on the President's demands.

This week, current and former State Department officials have begun cooperating with the impeachment inquiry by producing documents and scheduling interviews and depositions. Based on the first production of materials, it has become immediately apparent why Secretary Pompeo tried to block these officials from providing information.

The Committees have now obtained text messages from Ambassador Kurt Volker, the former Special Representative for Ukraine Negotiations, communicating with other officials, including William B. "Bill" Taylor, the Charge d'Affaires at the U.S. Embassy in Ukraine, Gordon Sondland, the U.S. Ambassador to the European Union, Andrey Yermak, Aide to Ukrainian President Zelensky, the President's agent Rudy Giuliani, and others.

These text messages reflect serious concerns raised by a State Department official about the detrimental effects of withholding critical military assistance from Ukraine, and the importance of setting up a meeting between President Trump and the Ukrainian President without further delay. He also directly expressed concerns that this critical military assistance and the meeting between the two presidents were being withheld in order to place additional pressure on Ukraine to deliver on the President's demand for Ukraine to launch politically motivated investigations.

Earlier today, selected portions of these texts were leaked to the press out of context. In order to help correct the public record, we are now providing an attachment with more complete excerpts from the exchanges. The additional excerpts we are providing are still only a subset of the full body of the materials, which we hope to make public after a review for personally identifiable information.

Our investigation will continue in the coming days. But we hope every Member of the House will join us in condemning in the strongest terms the President's now open defiance of our core values as American citizens to guard against foreign interference in our democratic process.

Sincerely,

Eliot L. Engel
Chairman
House Committee on Foreign Affairs

Adam B. Schiff
Chairman
House Permanent Select Committee
on Intelligence

Elijah E. Cummings
Chairman
House Committee on Oversight and Reform

ATTACHMENT

- **Connecting Rudy Giuliani with Ukraine President Zelensky's Advisor:** On July 19, Ambassador Volker texted President Trump's agent, Rudy Giuliani, to thank him for breakfast and to introduce him to Andrey Yermak, a top advisor to President Zelensky:

  > [7/19/19, 4:48 PM] Kurt Volker: Mr Mayor – really enjoyed breakfast this morning. As discussed, connecting you here with Andrey Yermak, who is very close to President Zelensky. I suggest we schedule a call together on Monday – maybe 10am or 11am Washington time? Kurt

- **Sondland Briefs Zelensky Ahead of Call with President Trump:** On July 19, 2019, Ambassador Volker, Ambassador Sondland, and Mr. Taylor had the following exchange about the specific goal for the upcoming telephone call between President Trump and the Ukrainian President:

  > [7/19/19, 4:49:42 PM] Kurt Volker: Can we three do a call tomorrow—say noon WASHINGTON?

  > [7/19/19, 6:50:29 PM] Gordon Sondland: Looks like Potus call tomorrow. I spike [sic] directly to Zelensky and gave him a full briefing. He's got it.

  > [7/19/19, 6:52:57 PM] Gordon Sondland: Sure!

  > [7/19/19, 7:01:22 PM] Kurt Volker: Good. Had breakfast with Rudy this morning—teeing up call w Yermak Monday. Must have helped. Most impt is for Zelensky to say that he will help investigation—and address any specific personnel issues—if there are any

- **Concerns about Ukraine Becoming an "Instrument" in U.S. Politics:** On July 21, 2019, Ambassador Taylor flagged President Zelensky's desire for Ukraine not to be used by the Trump Administration for its own domestic political purposes:

  > [7/21/19, 1:45:54 AM] Bill Taylor: Gordon, one thing Kurt and I talked about yesterday was Sasha Danyliuk's point that President Zelenskyy is sensitive about Ukraine being taken seriously, not merely as an instrument in Washington domestic, reelection politics.

  > [7/21/19, 4:45:44 AM] Gordon Sondland: Absolutely, but we need to get the conversation started and the relationship built, irrespective of the pretext. I am worried about the alternative.

- **Giuliani Advocates for Trump-Zelensky Call:** Mr. Yermak and Mr. Giuliani agreed to speak on the morning of July 22. Later that evening, Ambassador Volker informed Ambassadors Sondland and Taylor that Giuliani was now "advocating" for a phone call between President Trump and President Zelensky:

4

[7/22/19 4:27:55 PM] Kurt Volker: Orchestrated a great phone call w Rudy and Yermak. They are going to get together when Rudy goes to Madrid in a couple of weeks.

[7/22/19 4:28:08 PM] Kurt Volker: In the meantime Rudy is now advocating for phone call.

[7/22/19 4:28:26 PM] Kurt Volker: I have call into Fiona's replacement and will call Bolton if needed.

[7/22/19 4:28:48 PM Kurt Volker: But I can tell Bolton and you can tell Mick that Rudy agrees on a call if that helps.

[7/22/19 4:30:10 PM] Gordon Sondland: I talked to Tim Morrison Fiona's replacement. He is pushing but feel free as well.

- **Volker Advises Yermak Ahead of Trump-Zelensky Call:** On the morning of July 25, 2019—*ahead* of the planned call between President Trump and President Zelensky— Ambassador Volker advised Andrey Yermak:

  [7/25/19, 8:36:45 AM] Kurt Volker: Good lunch - thanks. Heard from White House—assuming President Z convinces trump he will investigate / "get to the bottom of what happened" in 2016, we will nail down date for visit to Washington. Good luck! See you tomorrow- kurt

- **Yermak's Informal Readout of the Trump-Zelensky Call:** Following President Trump's July 25 call, Ambassador Volker received the following readout from Ukrainian Presidential Advisor Yermak and confirmed his intent to meet Giuliani in Madrid:

  [7/25/19, 10:15:06 AM] Andrey Yermak: Phone call went well. President Trump proposed to choose any convenient dates. President Zelenskiy chose 20,21,22 September for the White House Visit. Thank you again for your help! Please remind Mr. Mayor to share the Madrid's dates

  [7/25/19, 10:16:42 AM] Kurt Volker: Great —thanks and will do!

- **State Department Officials Discuss a White House Visit and Ukraine Statement:** On August 9, 2019, Ambassador Volker had the following exchange with Ambassador Sondland about arranging a White House meeting after the Ukrainian President makes a public statement:

  [8/9/19, 5: 35:53 PM] Gordon Sondland: Morrison ready to get dates as soon as Yermak confirms.

  [8/9/19, 5: 46:21 PM] Kurt Volker: Excellent!! How did you sway him? :)

[8/9/19, 5: 47:34 PM] Gordon Sondland: Not sure i did. I think potus really wants the deliverable

[8/9/19, 5: 48:00 PM] Kurt Volker: But does he know that?

[8/9/19, 5: 48:09 PM] Gordon Sondland: Yep

[8/9/19, 5: 48:37 PM] Gordon Sondland: Clearly lots of convos going on

[8/9/19, 5:48:38 PM] Kurt Volker: Ok—then that's good it's coming from two separate sources

[8/9/19, 5: 51:18 PM] Gordon Sondland: To avoid misundestandings, might be helpful to ask Andrey for a draft statememt (embargoed) so that we can see exactly what they propose to cover. Even though Ze does a live presser they can still summarize in a brief statement. Thoughts?

[8/9/19, 5: 51:42 PM] Kurt Volker: Agree!

- **State Department Officials Seek Giuliani's Guidance on Ukraine Statement:** On August 9, 2019, after Mr. Giuliani met with President Zelensky's aide Andrey Yermak, Ambassador Volker asked to speak with Mr. Giuliani about the Ukranian statement:

   [8/9/19, 11:27 AM] Kurt Volker: Hi Mr Mayor! Had a good chat with Yermak last night. He was pleased with your phone call. Mentioned Z making a statement. Can we all get on the phone to make sure I advise Z correctly as to what he should be saying? Want to make sure we get this done right. Thanks!

   Gordon Sondland: Good idea Kurt. I am on Pacific time.

   Rudy Giuliani: Yes can you call now going to Fundraiser at 12:30

- **Ukrainian Aide Seeks White House Date First:** On August 10, 2019, President Zelensky's aide, Andrey Yermak, pressed Ambassador Volker for a date for the White House visit before committing to a statement announcing an investigation explicitly referencing the 2016 election and Burisma:

   [8/10/19, 4:56:15 PM] Andrey Yermak: Hi Kurt. Please let me know when you can talk. I think it's possible to make this declaration and mention all these things. Which we discussed yesterday. But it will be logic to do after we receive a confirmation of date. We inform about date of visit and about our expectations and our guarantees for future visit. Let discuss it

   [8/10/19, 5:01:32 PM] Kurt Volker: Ok! It's late for you—why don't we talk in my morning, your afternoon tomorrow? Say 10am/5pm?

> [8/10/19, 5:02:18 PM] Kurt Volker: I agree with your approach. Let's iron out statement and use that to get date and then PreZ can go forward with it?

> [8/10/19, 5:26:17 PM] Andrey Yermak: Ok

> [8/10/19, 5:38:43 PM] Kurt Volker: Great. Gordon is available to join as well

> [8/10/19, 5:41:45 PM] Andrey Yermak: Excellent

> [8/10/ 19, 5:42:10 PM] Andrey Yermak: Once we have a date, will call for a press briefing, announcing upcoming visit and outlining vision for the reboot of US-UKRAINE relationship, including among other things Burisma and election meddling in investigations

> [8/10/19, 5:42:30 PM] Kurt Volker: Sounds great!

- **Discussion of Ukrainian Statement to Include References to 2016 Election and Burisma:** Following the August 9, 2019, outreach to Rudy Giuliani, Ambassador Volker and Ambassador Sondland on August 13, 2019, had following exchange regarding the proposed Ukrainian statement:

> [8/13/19, 10:26:44 AM] Kurt Volker: Special attention should be paid to the problem of interference in the political processes of the United States especially with the alleged involvement of some Ukrainian politicians. I want to declare that this is unacceptable. We intend to initiate and complete a transparent and unbiased investigation of all available facts and episodes, including those involving Burisma and the 2016 U.S. elections, which in turn will prevent the recurrence of this problem in the future.

> [8/13/19, 10:27:20 AM] Gordon Sondland: Perfect. Lets send to Andrey after our call

- **Confirming Desire to Reference 2016 Election and Burisma:** On August 17, 2019, Ambassadors Volker and Sondland had the following exchange in which they discussed their message to Ukraine:

> [8/17/19, 3:06:19 PM] Gordon Sondland: Do we still want Ze to give us an unequivocal draft with 2016 and Boresma?

> [8/17/19, 4:34:21 PM] Kurt Volker: That's the clear message so far …

> [8/17/19, 4:34:39 PM] Kurt Volker: I'm hoping we can put something out there that causes him to respond with that

> [8/17/19, 4:41:09 PM] Gordon Sondland: Unless you think otherwise I will return Andreys call tomorrow and suggest they send us a clean draft.

7

- **Ukrainian Official Shares Press Report of U.S. Withholding Military Assistance:**
  On August 28, President Zelensky's aide, Andrey Yermak, texted Ambassador Volker a
  news story entitled, "Trump Holds Up Ukraine Military Aid Meant to Confront Russia":

  > [8/29/19, 2:28:19 AM] Andrey Yermak: Need to talk with you

  > [8/29/19, 3:06:14 AM] Andrey Yermak:
  > https://www.politico.com/story/2019/08/28/trump-ukraine-military-aid-russia-
  > 1689531

  > [8/29/19, 6:55:04 AM] Kurt Volker: Hi Andrey – absolutely. When is good for
  > you?

- **President Trump Cancels Trip to Meet President Zelensky:** On August 30,
  Ambassador Taylor informed Ambassador Volker that President Trump had canceled his
  planned visit to Warsaw, Poland, where he was to meet with President Zelensky.
  Ambassadors Volker and Sondland discussed an alternative plan for Vice President
  Pence to meet with President Zelensky on September 1:

  > [8/30/19, 12:14:57 AM] Bill Taylor: Trip canceled

  > [8/30/19, 12:16:02 AM] Kurt Volker: Hope VPOTUS keeps the bilat – and tees
  > up WH visit…

  > [8/30/19, 12:16:18 AM] Kurt Volker: And hope Gordon and Perry still going…

  > [8/30/19, 5:31:14 AM] Gordon Sondland: I am going. Pompeo is speaking to
  > Potus today to see if he can go.

  On September 1, Ambassador Taylor sought clarification of the requirements for a White
  House visit:

  > [9/1/19, 12:08:57 PM] Bill Taylor: Are we now saying that security assistance
  > and WH meeting are conditioned on investigations?

  > [9/1/19, 12:42:29 PM] Gordon Sondland: Call me

- **State Department Officials on Security Assistance and the Ukraine "Interview":** On
  September 8, Ambassador Taylor, Ambassador Sondland, and Ambassador Volker had
  the following exchange:

  > [9/8/19, 11:20:32 AM] Gordon Sondland: Guys multiple convos with Ze, Potus.
  > Lets talk

  > [9/8/19, 11:21:41 AM] Bill Taylor: Now is fine with me

8

[9/8/19, 11:26:13 AM] Kurt Volker: Try again—could not hear

[9/8/19, 11:40:11 AM] Bill Taylor: Gordon and I just spoke. I can brief you if you and Gordon don't connect

[9/8/19, 12:37:28 PM] Bill Taylor: The nightmare is they give the interview and don't get the security assistance. The Russians love it. (And I quit.)

- **State Department Officials on Withholding Security Assistance**: On September 9, 2019, Ambassador Taylor and Ambassador Sondland had the following exchange regarding the withholding of military assistance to Ukraine:

  [9/9/19, 12:31:06 AM] Bill Taylor: The message to the Ukrainians (and Russians) we send with the decision on security assistance is key. With the hold, we have already shaken their faith in us. Thus my nightmare scenario.

  [9/9/19, 12:34:44 AM] Bill Taylor: Counting on you to be right about this interview, Gordon.

  [9/9/19, 12:37:16 AM] Gordon Sondland: Bill, I never said I was "right". I said we are where we are and believe we have identified the best pathway forward. Lets hope it works.

  [9/9/19, 12:47:11 AM] Bill Taylor: As I said on the phone, I think it's crazy to withhold security assistance for help with a political campaign.

  [9/9/19, 5:19:35 AM] Gordon Sondland: Bill, I believe you are incorrect about President Trump's intentions. The President has been crystal clear no quid pro quo's of any kind. The President is trying to evaluate whether Ukraine is truly going to adopt the transparency and reforms that President Zelensky promised during his campaign I suggest we stop the back and forth by text If you still have concerns I recommend you give Lisa Kenna or S a call to discuss them directly. Thanks.

THE WHITE HOUSE LETTER

THE WHITE HOUSE

WASHINGTON

October 8, 2019

The Honorable Nancy Pelosi
Speaker
House of Representatives
Washington, D.C. 20515

The Honorable Eliot L. Engel
Chairman
House Foreign Affairs Committee
Washington, D.C. 20515

The Honorable Adam B. Schiff
Chairman
House Permanent Select Committee on
Intelligence
Washington, D.C. 20515

The Honorable Elijah E. Cummings
Chairman
House Committee on Oversight and Reform
Washington, D.C. 20515

Dear Madam Speaker and Messrs. Chairmen:

I write on behalf of President Donald J. Trump in response to your numerous, legally unsupported demands made as part of what you have labeled—contrary to the Constitution of the United States and all past bipartisan precedent—as an "impeachment inquiry." As you know, you have designed and implemented your inquiry in a manner that violates fundamental fairness and constitutionally mandated due process.

For example, you have denied the President the right to cross-examine witnesses, to call witnesses, to receive transcripts of testimony, to have access to evidence, to have counsel present, and many other basic rights guaranteed to all Americans. You have conducted your proceedings in secret. You have violated civil liberties and the separation of powers by threatening Executive Branch officials, claiming that you will seek to punish those who exercise fundamental constitutional rights and prerogatives. All of this violates the Constitution, the rule of law, and *every past precedent*. Never before in our history has the House of Representatives—under the control of either political party—taken the American people down the dangerous path you seem determined to pursue.

Put simply, you seek to overturn the results of the 2016 election and deprive the American people of the President they have freely chosen. Many Democrats now apparently view impeachment not only as a means to undo the democratic results of the *last* election, but as a strategy to influence the *next* election, which is barely more than a year away. As one member of Congress explained, he is "concerned that if we don't impeach the President, he will get reelected."[1] Your highly partisan and unconstitutional effort threatens grave and lasting damage to our democratic institutions, to our system of free elections, and to the American people.

---

[1] Interview with Rep. Al Green, MSNBC (May 5, 2019).

Speaker Pelosi, and Chairmen Engel, Schiff, and
Cummings
Page 2

For his part, President Trump took the unprecedented step of providing the public
transparency by declassifying and releasing the record of his call with President Zelenskyy of
Ukraine. The record clearly established that the call was completely appropriate and that there is
no basis for your inquiry. The fact that there was nothing wrong with the call was also
powerfully confirmed by Chairman Schiff's decision to create a false version of the call and read
it to the American people at a congressional hearing, without disclosing that he was simply
making it all up.

In addition, information has recently come to light that the whistleblower had contact
with Chairman Schiff's office before filing the complaint. His initial denial of such contact
caused *The Washington Post* to conclude that Chairman Schiff "clearly made a statement that
was false."[2] In any event, the American people understand that Chairman Schiff cannot covertly
assist with the submission of a complaint, mislead the public about his involvement, read a
counterfeit version of the call to the American people, and then pretend to sit in judgment as a
neutral "investigator."

For these reasons, President Trump and his Administration reject your baseless,
unconstitutional efforts to overturn the democratic process. Your unprecedented actions have
left the President with no choice. In order to fulfill his duties to the American people, the
Constitution, the Executive Branch, and all future occupants of the Office of the Presidency,
President Trump and his Administration cannot participate in your partisan and unconstitutional
inquiry under these circumstances.

I.   Your "Inquiry" Is Constitutionally Invalid and Violates Basic Due Process Rights and the Separation of Powers.

Your inquiry is constitutionally invalid and a violation of due process. In the history of
our Nation, the House of Representatives has never attempted to launch an impeachment inquiry
against the President without a majority of the House taking political accountability for that
decision by voting to authorize such a dramatic constitutional step. Here, House leadership
claims to have initiated the gravest inter-branch conflict contemplated under our Constitution by
means of nothing more than a press conference at which the Speaker of the House simply
announced an "official impeachment inquiry."[3] Your contrived process is unprecedented in the

---

[2]   Glenn Kessler, *Schiff's False Claim His Committee Had Not Spoken to the Whistleblower*, Wash. Post (Oct. 4, 2019).

[3]   Press Release, Nancy Pelosi, Pelosi Remarks Announcing Impeachment Inquiry (Sept. 24, 2019).

Speaker Pelosi, and Chairmen Engel, Schiff, and
Cummings
Page 3

history of the Nation,[4] and lacks the necessary authorization for a valid impeachment
proceeding.[5]

The Committees' inquiry also suffers from a separate, fatal defect. Despite Speaker
Pelosi's commitment to "treat the President with fairness,"[6] the Committees have not established
any procedures affording the President even the most basic protections demanded by due process
under the Constitution and by fundamental fairness. Chairman Nadler of the House Judiciary
Committee has expressly acknowledged, at least when the President was a member of his own
party, that "[t]he power of impeachment . . . demands a rigorous level of due process," and that
in this context "due process mean[s] . . . the right to be informed of the law, of the charges
against you, the right to confront the witnesses against you, to call your own witnesses, and to
have the assistance of counsel."[7] All of these procedures have been abandoned here.

These due process rights are not a matter of discretion for the Committees to dispense
with at will. To the contrary, they are constitutional requirements. The Supreme Court has
recognized that due process protections apply to all congressional investigations.[8] Indeed, it has
been recognized that the Due Process Clause applies to impeachment proceedings.[9] And
precedent for the rights to cross-examine witnesses, call witnesses, and present evidence dates
back nearly 150 years.[10] Yet the Committees have decided to deny the President these
elementary rights and protections that form the basis of the American justice system and are
protected by the Constitution. No citizen—including the President—should be treated this
unfairly.

---

[4] Since the Founding of the Republic, under unbroken practice, the House has never undertaken the solemn
responsibility of an impeachment inquiry directed at the President without first adopting a resolution authorizing
a committee to begin the inquiry. The inquiries into the impeachments of Presidents Andrew Johnson and Bill
Clinton proceeded in multiple phases, each authorized by a separate House resolution. *See, e.g.,* H.R. Res. 581,
105th Cong. (1998); H.R. Res. 525, 105th Cong. (1998); III Hinds' Precedents §§ 2400-02, 2408, 2412. And
before the Judiciary Committee initiated an impeachment inquiry into President Richard Nixon, the Committee's
chairman rightfully recognized that "a[n] [inquiry] resolution has always been passed by the House" and "is a
necessary step." III Deschler's Precedents ch. 14, § 15.2. The House then satisfied that requirement by adopting
H.R. Res. 803, 93rd Cong. (1974).

[5] Chairman Nadler has recognized the importance of taking a vote in the House before beginning a presidential
impeachment inquiry. At the outset of the Clinton impeachment inquiry—where a floor vote was held—he
argued that even limiting the time for *debate* before that vote was improper and that "an hour debate on this
momentous decision is an insult to the American people and another sign that this is not going to be fair." 144
Cong. Rec. H10018 (daily ed. Oct. 8, 1998) (statement of Rep. Jerrold Nadler). Here, the House has dispensed
with any vote and any debate *at all.*

[6] Press Release, Nancy Pelosi, Transcript of Pelosi Weekly Press Conference Today (Oct. 2, 2019).

[7] *Examining the Allegations of Misconduct Against IRS Commissioner John Koskinen (Part II): Hearing Before
the H. Comm. on the Judiciary,* 114th Cong. 3 (2016) (statement of Rep. Jerrold Nadler); *Background and
History of Impeachment: Hearing Before the Subcomm. on the Constitution of the H. Comm. on the Judiciary,*
105th Cong. 17 (1998) (statement of Rep. Jerrold Nadler).

[8] *See, e.g., Watkins v. United States,* 354 U.S. 178, 188 (1957); *Quinn v. United States,* 349 U.S. 155, 161 (1955).

[9] *See Hastings v. United States,* 802 F. Supp. 490, 504 (D.D.C. 1992), *vacated on other grounds by Hastings v.
United States,* 988 F.2d 1280 (D.C. Cir. 1993).

[10] *See, e.g.,* III Hinds' Precedents § 2445.

Speaker Pelosi, and Chairmen Engel, Schiff, and
Cummings
Page 4

To comply with the Constitution's demands, appropriate procedures would include—at a minimum—the right to see all evidence, to present evidence, to call witnesses, to have counsel present at all hearings, to cross-examine all witnesses, to make objections relating to the examination of witnesses or the admissibility of testimony and evidence, and to respond to evidence and testimony. Likewise, the Committees must provide for the disclosure of all evidence favorable to the President and all evidence bearing on the credibility of witnesses called to testify in the inquiry. The Committees' current procedures provide *none* of these basic constitutional rights.

In addition, the House has not provided the Committees' Ranking Members with the authority to issue subpoenas. The right of the minority to issue subpoenas—subject to the same rules as the majority—has been the standard, bipartisan practice in all recent resolutions authorizing presidential impeachment inquiries.[11] The House's failure to provide co-equal subpoena power in this case ensures that any inquiry will be nothing more than a one-sided effort by House Democrats to gather information favorable to their views and to selectively release it as only they determine. The House's utter disregard for the established procedural safeguards followed in past impeachment inquiries shows that the current proceedings are nothing more than an unconstitutional exercise in political theater.

As if denying the President basic procedural protections were not enough, the Committees have also resorted to threats and intimidation against potential Executive Branch witnesses. Threats by the Committees against Executive Branch witnesses who assert common and longstanding rights destroy the integrity of the process and brazenly violate fundamental due process. In letters to State Department employees, the Committees have ominously threatened—without any legal basis and before the Committees even issued a subpoena—that "[a]ny failure to appear" in response to a mere letter *request* for a deposition "shall constitute evidence of obstruction."[12] Worse, the Committees have broadly threatened that if State Department officials attempt to insist upon the right for the Department to have an agency lawyer present at depositions to protect legitimate Executive Branch confidentiality interests—or apparently if they make any effort to protect those confidentiality interests *at all*—these officials will have their salaries withheld.[13]

The suggestion that it would somehow be problematic for anyone to raise long-established Executive Branch confidentiality interests and privileges in response to a request for a deposition is legally unfounded. Not surprisingly, the Office of Legal Counsel at the Department of Justice has made clear on multiple occasions that employees of the Executive Branch who have been instructed not to appear or not to provide particular testimony before Congress based on privileges or immunities of the Executive Branch cannot be punished for

---

[11] H.R. Res. 581, 105th Cong. (1998); H.R. Res. 803, 93rd Cong. (1974).

[12] Letter from Eliot L. Engel, Chairman, House Committee on Foreign Affairs, et al., to George P. Kent, Deputy Assistant Secretary, U.S. Department of State 1 (Sept. 27, 2019).

[13] *See* Letter from Eliot L. Engel, Chairman, House Committee on Foreign Affairs, et al., to John J. Sullivan, Deputy Secretary of State 2-3 (Oct. 1, 2019).

Speaker Pelosi, and Chairmen Engel, Schiff, and
Cummings
Page 5

following such instructions.[14] Current and former State Department officials are duty bound to
protect the confidentiality interests of the Executive Branch, and the Office of Legal Counsel has
also recognized that it is unconstitutional to exclude agency counsel from participating in
congressional depositions.[15] In addition, any attempt to withhold an official's salary for the
assertion of such interests would be unprecedented and unconstitutional.[16] The Committees'
assertions on these points amount to nothing more than strong-arm tactics designed to rush
proceedings without any regard for due process and the rights of individuals and of the Executive
Branch. Threats aimed at intimidating individuals who assert these basic rights are attacks on
civil liberties that should profoundly concern all Americans.

**II.   The Invalid "Impeachment Inquiry" Plainly Seeks To Reverse the Election of 2016
         and To Influence the Election of 2020.**

         The effort to impeach President Trump—without regard to any evidence of his actions in
office—is a naked political strategy that began the day he was inaugurated, and perhaps even
before.[17] In fact, your transparent rush to judgment, lack of democratically accountable
authorization, and violation of basic rights in the current proceedings make clear the illegitimate,
partisan purpose of this purported "impeachment inquiry." The Founders, however, did not
create the extraordinary mechanism of impeachment so it could be used by a political party that
feared for its prospects against the sitting President in the next election. The decision as to who
will be elected President in 2020 should rest with the people of the United States, exactly where
the Constitution places it.

         Democrats themselves used to recognize the dire implications of impeachment for the
Nation. For example, in the past, Chairman Nadler has explained:

         The effect of impeachment is to overturn the popular will of the voters. We
         must not overturn an election and remove a President from office except to
         defend our system of government or our constitutional liberties against a dire
         threat, and we must not do so without an overwhelming consensus of the
         American people. There must never be a narrowly voted impeachment or an
         impeachment supported by one of our major political parties and opposed by
         another. Such an impeachment will produce divisiveness and bitterness in our

---

[14] *See, e.g., Testimonial Immunity Before Congress of the Former Counsel to the President*, 43 Op. O.L.C. __, *19
(May 20, 2019); *Prosecution for Contempt of Congress of an Executive Branch Official Who Has Asserted a
Claim of Executive Privilege*, 8 Op. O.L.C. 101, 102, 140 (1984) ("The Executive, however, must be free from
the threat of criminal prosecution if its right to assert executive privilege is to have any practical substance.")

[15] *Attempted Exclusion of Agency Counsel from Congressional Depositions of Agency Employees*, 43 Op. O.L.C.
__, *1-2 (May 23, 2019).

[16] *See* President Donald J. Trump, Statement by the President on Signing the Consolidated Appropriations Act,
2019 (Feb. 15, 2019); *Authority of Agency Officials To Prohibit Employees From Providing Information to
Congress*, 28 Op. O.L.C. 79, 80 (2004).

[17] *See* Matea Gold, *The Campaign To Impeach President Trump Has Begun*, Wash. Post (Jan. 21, 2017) ("At the
moment the new commander in chief was sworn in, a campaign to build public support for his impeachment
went live . . . .").

Speaker Pelosi, and Chairmen Engel, Schiff, and
Cummings
Page 6

politics for years to come, and will call into question the very legitimacy of
our political institutions.[18]

Unfortunately, the President's political opponents now seem eager to transform
impeachment from an extraordinary remedy that should rarely be contemplated into a
conventional political weapon to be deployed for partisan gain. These actions are a far cry from
what our Founders envisioned when they vested Congress with the "important trust" of
considering impeachment.[19] Precisely because it nullifies the outcome of the democratic
process, impeachment of the President is fraught with the risk of deepening divisions in the
country and creating long-lasting rifts in the body politic.[20] Unfortunately, you are now playing
out exactly the partisan rush to judgment that the Founders so strongly warned against. The
American people deserve much better than this.

III. There Is No Legitimate Basis for Your "Impeachment Inquiry"; Instead, the Committees' Actions Raise Serious Questions.

It is transparent that you have resorted to such unprecedented and unconstitutional
procedures because you know that a fair process would expose the lack of any basis for your
inquiry. Your current effort is founded on a completely appropriate call on July 25, 2019,
between President Trump and President Zelenskyy of Ukraine. Without waiting to see what was
actually said on the call, a press conference was held announcing an "impeachment inquiry"
based on falsehoods and misinformation about the call.[21] To rebut those falsehoods, and to
provide transparency to the American people, President Trump secured agreement from the
Government of Ukraine and took the extraordinary step of declassifying and publicly releasing
the record of the call. That record clearly established that the call was completely appropriate,
that the President did nothing wrong, and that there is no basis for an impeachment inquiry. At a
joint press conference shortly after the call's public release, President Zelenskyy agreed that the
call was appropriate.[22] In addition, the Department of Justice announced that officials there had
reviewed the call after a referral for an alleged campaign finance law violation and found no such
violation.[23]

Perhaps the best evidence that there was no wrongdoing on the call is the fact that, after
the actual record of the call was released, Chairman Schiff chose to concoct a false version of the
call and to read his made-up transcript to the American people at a public hearing.[24] This

---

[18] 144 Cong. Rec. H11786 (daily ed. Dec. 18, 1998) (statement of Rep. Jerrold Nadler).

[19] The Federalist No. 65 (Alexander Hamilton).

[20] *See id.*

[21] Press Release, Nancy Pelosi, Pelosi Remarks Announcing Impeachment Inquiry (Sept. 24, 2019).

[22] *President Trump Meeting with Ukrainian President*, C-SPAN (Sept. 25, 2019).

[23] Statement of Kerri Kupec, Director, Office of Public Affairs, Dept. of Justice (Sept. 25, 2019) ("[T]he Department's Criminal Division reviewed the official record of the call and determined, based on the facts and applicable law, that there was no campaign finance violation and that no further action was warranted.").

[24] *See Whistleblower Disclosure: Hearing Before the H. Select Comm. on Intel.*, 116th Cong. (Sept. 26, 2019) (statement of Rep. Adam Schiff).

Speaker Pelosi, and Chairmen Engel, Schiff, and
Cummings
Page 7

powerfully confirms there is no issue with the actual call. Otherwise, why would Chairman
Schiff feel the need to make up his own version? The Chairman's action only further
undermines the public's confidence in the fairness of any inquiry before his Committee.

The real problem, as we are now learning, is that Chairman Schiff's office, and perhaps
others—despite initial denials—were involved in advising the whistleblower before the
complaint was filed. Initially, when asked on national television about interactions with the
whistleblower, Chairman Schiff unequivocally stated that "[w]e have not spoken directly with
the whistleblower. We would like to."[25]

Now, however, it has been reported that the whistleblower approached the House
Intelligence Committee with information—and received guidance from the Committee—*before*
filing a complaint with the Inspector General.[26] As a result, *The Washington Post* concluded that
Chairman Schiff "clearly made a statement that was false."[27] Anyone who was involved in the
preparation or submission of the whistleblower's complaint cannot possibly act as a fair and
impartial judge in the same matter—particularly after misleading the American people about his
involvement.

All of this raises serious questions that must be investigated. However, the Committees
are preventing anyone, including the minority, from looking into these critically important
matters. At the very least, Chairman Schiff must immediately make available all documents
relating to these issues. After all, the American people have a right to know about the
Committees' own actions with respect to these matters.

*   *   *

Given that your inquiry lacks any legitimate constitutional foundation, any pretense of
fairness, or even the most elementary due process protections, the Executive Branch cannot be
expected to participate in it. Because participating in this inquiry under the current
unconstitutional posture would inflict lasting institutional harm on the Executive Branch and
lasting damage to the separation of powers, you have left the President no choice. Consistent
with the duties of the President of the United States, and in particular his obligation to preserve
the rights of future occupants of his office, President Trump cannot permit his Administration to
participate in this partisan inquiry under these circumstances.

Your recent letter to the Acting White House Chief of Staff argues that "[e]ven if an
impeachment inquiry were not underway," the Oversight Committee may seek this information

---

[25] Interview with Chairman Adam Schiff, MSNBC (Sept. 17, 2019).

[26] Julian Barnes, et al., *Schiff Got Early Account of Accusations as Whistle-Blower's Concerns Grew*, N.Y. Times
(Oct. 2, 2019).

[27] Glenn Kessler, *Schiff's False Claim His Committee Had Not Spoken to the Whistleblower*, Wash. Post (Oct. 4,
2019).

Speaker Pelosi, and Chairmen Engel, Schiff, and
Cummings
Page 8

as a matter of the established oversight process.[28] Respectfully, the Committees cannot have it
both ways. The letter comes from the Chairmen of three different Committees, it transmits a
subpoena "[p]ursuant to the House of Representatives' impeachment inquiry," it recites that the
documents will "be collected as part of the House's impeachment inquiry," and it asserts that the
documents will be "shared among the Committees, as well as with the Committee on the
Judiciary as appropriate."[29] The letter is in no way directed at collecting information in aid of
legislation, and you simply cannot expect to rely on oversight authority to gather information for
an unauthorized impeachment inquiry that conflicts with all historical precedent and rides
roughshod over due process and the separation of powers. If the Committees wish to return to
the regular order of oversight requests, we stand ready to engage in that process as we have in
the past, in a manner consistent with well-established bipartisan constitutional protections and a
respect for the separation of powers enshrined in our Constitution.

For the foregoing reasons, the President cannot allow your constitutionally illegitimate
proceedings to distract him and those in the Executive Branch from their work on behalf of the
American people. The President has a country to lead. The American people elected him to do
this job, and he remains focused on fulfilling his promises to the American people. He has
important work that he must continue on their behalf, both at home and around the world,
including continuing strong economic growth, extending historically low levels of
unemployment, negotiating trade deals, fixing our broken immigration system, lowering
prescription drug prices, and addressing mass shooting violence. We hope that, in light of the
many deficiencies we have identified in your proceedings, you will abandon the current invalid
efforts to pursue an impeachment inquiry and join the President in focusing on the many
important goals that matter to the American people.

Sincerely,

Pat A. Cipollone
Counsel to the President

cc: Hon. Kevin McCarthy, Minority Leader, House of Representatives
       Hon. Michael McCaul, Ranking Member, House Committee on Foreign Affairs
       Hon. Devin Nunes, Ranking Member, House Permanent Select Committee on
       Intelligence
       Hon. Jim Jordan, Ranking Member, House Committee on Oversight and Reform

---

[28] Letter from Elijah E. Cummings, Chairman, House Committee on Oversight and Government Reform, et al., to
John Michael Mulvaney, Acting Chief of Staff to the President 3 (Oct. 4, 2019).

[29] *Id.* at 1.

Notes

Introduction

page

2   *Five minutes and 21 seconds:* James M. Naughton. "A Historic Charge." *New York Times,* July 28, 1974. https://www.nytimes.com/1974/07/28/archives/a-historic-charge-two-more-articles.html.

    The vote came more than two years: Jilian Fama, and Meghan Kiesel. "Watergate Burglars: Where Are They Now?" ABC News, June 17, 2012. https://abcnews.go.com/Politics/watergate-burglars-now/story?id=16567157.

    In a Washington Post *article:* Richard Lyons, and William Chapman. "Judiciary Committee Approves Article to Impeach President Nixon." *Washington Post,* July 28, 1974. https://www.washingtonpost.com/wp-srv/national/longterm/watergate/articles/072874-1.htm.

3   *"I don't want to talk to anybody":* Ibid.

    Representative Walter Flowers: Ibid.

6   *Only two presidents in our nation's history:* Tara Law. "What to Know About the U.S. Presidents Who've Been Impeached." *Time,* September 29, 2019. https://time.com/5552679/impeached-presidents/.

    Only 19 officials: United States House of Representatives. "List of Individuals Impeached by the House of Representatives," n.d. https://history.house.gov/Institution/Impeachment/Impeachment-List/.

    As James Madison wrote: James Madison. *Federalist No. 51,* February 8, 1788.

9   *As Alexander Hamilton wrote:* Alexander Hamilton. *Federalist No. 65,* March 7, 1788.

    In one of the greatest speeches: George Washington. "Farewell Address." September 19, 1796.

    Similarly, John Adams: John Adams. "Letter to Thomas Jefferson," December 7, 1787. https://founders.archives.gov/documents/Adams/99-02-02-0281.

And when James Madison: Michael Sozan. "The Founders Would Have Impeached Trump for His Ukraine-Related Misconduct," September 26, 2019. https://www.americanprogress.org/issues/democracy/news/2019/09/26/475114/founders-impeached-trump-ukraine-related-misconduct/.

In 2008, a congressmen captured: Ari Melber. "Mike Pence Address to Congress on Impeachment." *Twitter.* October 9, 2019. https://twitter.com/TheBeatWith Ari/status/1182058746782068737.

11   *Whereas Mueller's report:* "Read the Transcript of Trump's Conversation with Volodymyr Zelensky — CNNPolitics," CNN.com, September 26, 2019, https://www.cnn.com/2019/09/25/politics/donald-trump-ukraine-transcript-call/index.html.

And we have a transcript: Katherine Faulders, and Conor Finnegan, *ABC News,* "'Crazy to Withhold Security Assistance' to Ukraine for Political Campaign: Top US Diplomat," October 3, 2019. https://abcnews.go.com/Politics/top-diplomat-ukraine-crazy-withhold-security-sasistance-political/story?id=66039011.

Acting White House chief of staff: Aaron Blake, "Analysis | Trump's Acting Chief of Staff Admits It: There Was a Ukraine Quid pro Quo," *Washington Post,* October 17, 2019, https://www.washingtonpost.com/politics/2019/10/17/white-house-chief-staff-mick-mulvaney-admits-it-there-was-ukraine-quid-pro-quo/.

12   *Moreover, not only do we have transcripts:* Donald Trump. "Twitter Post." *Twitter* (blog), October 3, 2019. https://twitter.com/realdonaldtrump/status/1179925259417468928?lang=en.

And he's doubling down: Kevin Breuninger, "Trump Says China Should Investigate the Bidens, Doubles down on Ukraine Probe," CNBC, October 3, 2019, https://www.cnbc.com/2019/10/03/trump-calls-for-ukraine-china-to-investigate-the-bidens.html.

This is the approach: Philip Bump. "If Trump Shot Someone Dead on Fifth Avenue, Many Supporters Would Call His Murder Trial Biased." *Washington Post,* March 14, 2019. https://www.washingtonpost.com/politics/2019/03/14/if-trump-shot-someone-dead-fifth-avenue-many-supporters-would-call-his-murder-trial-biased/.

13   *As Edmund Randolph said:* Erick Trickey, "Inside the Founding Fathers' Debate over what Constituted an Impeachable Offense," *Smithsonian Magazine,* October 2, 2017, https://www.smithsonianmag.com/history/inside-founding-fathers-debate-over-what-constituted-impeachable-offense-180965083/.

To crystallize this point: "Great Interviews of the 20th Century: Richard Nixon Interviewed by David Frost," *The Guardian,* September 7, 2007, sec. Media, https://www.theguardian.com/theguardian/2007/sep/07/greatinterviews1.

1. A Brief History of Impeachment

18   *After the soaring rhetoric:* Thomas Jefferson et al. "The Declaration of Independence," July 4, 1776. http://www.ushistory.org/declaration/document/.

"The executive will be": "Madison Debates."

19   *And, to create what James Madison:* Federalist No. 51.
      The Constitutional Convention: Jill Lepore. "How Impeachment Ended Up in the Constitution." *The New Yorker,* May 18, 2017. https://www.newyorker.com/news/news-desk/how-impeachment-ended-up-in-the-constitution.
      On that hot summer day: "Madison Debates"; Jill Lepore, "How Impeachment Ended Up in the Constitution."

20   *"Shall any man be":* "Madison Debates."
      The president, Madison warned: Ibid.
      William Richardson Davie: Jon Meacham, Peter Baker, Timothy Naftali, and Jeffrey A. Engel. *Impeachment: An American History.* Random House, 2018, p. 29.
      The debate went on: Jill Lepore: "How Impeachment Ended Up in the Constitution."

21   *But while King had a point:* "Madison Debates."
      as tensions grew between those: Ibid.
      While Franklin understood: Ibid.
      By the end of the day: Jill Lepore, "How Impeachment Ended Up in the Constitution."

22   *The king of England:* Erick Trickey. "Inside the Founding Fathers' Debate Over What Constituted an Impeachable Offense."
      Only if two-thirds: Charlie Savage. "How the Impeachment Process Works," *New York Times,* October 4, 2019. https://www.nytimes.com/2019/09/24/us/politics/impeachment-trump-explained.html.
      While Parliament could only impeach: Charles L. Black, and Philip Bobbitt. *Impeachment: A Handbook.* Yale University Press, 1974. pp. 117–118.

23   *And unlike in Britain:* United States Constitution, Article I, Section 3.
      As the convention wound down: John R. Vile. "The Critical Role of Committees at the U.S. Constitutional Convention of 1787." *The American Journal of Legal History* 28, no. 2 (April 2006): pp. 147–76.
      In early drafts of the Constitution: Trickey, "Inside the Founding Fathers' Debate over what Constituted an Impeachable Offense."
      Less than a week later: Ibid.
      The Constitution's definition of treason: United States Constitution, Article III, Section 3.

24   *Mason's suggestion:* "Madison Debates."
      Madison, one of the members: Erick Trickey, "Inside the Founding Fathers' Debate Over What Constituted an Impeachable Offense."
      "So vague a term": "Madison Debates."
      Mason conceded Madison's point: Ibid.
      The committee voted 8–3: Ibid.
      This Committee on Style: John R. Vile, "The Critical Role of Committees at the U.S. Constitutional Convention of 1787."

25   *They simply made the phrase:* "Madison Debates."

26   *According to the Constitution:* United States Constitution, Article III, Section 2.

This is an extreme case: Charles L. Black and Philip Bobbitt, *Impeachment: A Handbook,* p. 108.

27   *Or, as they write:* Ibid., p. 109.

After all, the very first federal official: Ezra Klein, "Impeachment Explained, Episode 1," Vox podcast, October 18, 2019.

28   *In the important presidential caucus:* "IA Code § 192.143," accessed October 24, 2019, https://law.justia.com/codes/iowa/2011/titlev/subtitle4/chapter 192/192-143/.

We know this interpretation: Charles L. Black and Philip Bobbitt, *Impeachment: A Handbook,* p. 110.

The severity of the crime: Jon Meacham et al., *Impeachment: An American History,* p. 110.

29   *Violating the Tenure of Office Act:* Charles L. Black and Philip Bobbitt, *Impeachment: A Handbook.*

The Supreme Court eventually ruled the Tenure Act: Ibid.

30   *The House voted to impeach:* Andrew Glass, "House votes to impeach Andrew Johnson, February 24, 1868," Politico, February 24, 2015, https://www.politico.com/story/2015/02/this-day-in-politics-115420.

An abolitionist senator from Kansas: Edmund Ross, Robert L. Jackson. "Impeach Vote Costly for Senator." *Los Angeles Times,* December 19, 1998. https://www.latimes.com/archives/la-xpm-1998-dec-19-mn-55589-story.html.

Far from it: Kansas Historical Society. "Edmund G. Ross Collection," n.d. https://www.kshs.org/p/edmund-g-ross-collection/14112.

For nearly a century: John F. Kennedy. *Profiles in Courage,* Harper & Row, 1955.

In a lonely grave: John F Kennedy Presidential Library and Museum, Part 3, Chapter 6: Edmund G. Ross:, https://www.jfklibrary.org/asset-viewer/archives/JFKPP/028/JFKPP-028-043.

31   *The story of President Clinton's impeachment:* Laurence Tribe, and Joshua Matz. *To End a Presidency: The Power of Impeachment.* Basic Books, 2018.

There is no denying: Bill Clinton: "I Did Not Have Sexual Relations with That Woman," accessed October 24, 2019, https://www.washingtonpost.com/video/politics/bill-clinton-i-did-not-have-sexual-relations-with-that-woman/2018/01/25/4a953c22-0221-11e8-86b9-8908743c79dd_video.html; "The Impeachment of Bill Clinton," *Bill of Rights Institute* (blog), accessed October 24, 2019, https://billofrightsinstitute.org/elessons/the-impeachment-of-bill-clinton/.

32   *Tribe and Joshua Matz write:* Laurence Tribe and Joshua Matz, *To End a Presidency: The Power of Impeachment,* p. 21.

As Jeffrey A. Engel writes: Jon Meacham et al., *Impeachment: An American History,* pp. xiii–xiv.

33   *This played out most explicitly:* Ronald G. Shafer. "'He Lies like a Dog': The First Effort to Impeach a President Was Led by His Own Party." *Washington Post,* September 23, 2019. https://www.washingtonpost.com/history/2019/09/23/he-lies-like-dog-first-effort-impeach-president-was-led-by-his-own-party/.

This worried Whigs in Congress: Ibid.

In July of 1842: United States House of Representatives. "A Petition for a Presidential Impeachment," n.d. https://history.house.gov/HistoricalHighlight/Detail/15032448949.

"If the power of impeachment": Ronald G. Shafer, "'He Lies like a Dog': The First Effort to Impeach a President Was Led by His Own Party."

34 *let him serve out:* Ibid.

35 *It was the intention:* United States Constitutional Convention. *The Records of the Federal Convention of 1787.* Edited by Max Farrand. Vol. III. Yale University Press, 1911, p. 268.

This is why: Alexander Hamilton. *Federalist No. 65.* March 7, 1788.

The midnight to 7 a.m.: DeNeen L. Brown. "'The Post' and the Forgotten Security Guard Who Discovered the Watergate Break-In." *Washington Post,* December 22, 2017. https://www.washingtonpost.com/news/retropolis/wp/2017/12/22/the-post-and-the-forgotten-security-guard-who-discovered-the-watergate-break-in/.

36 *But late in the night:* The Impeachment of Richard Nixon, Tom van der Voort, "Watergate: The Break-In," Miller Center, June 6, 2017, https://millercenter.org/the-presidency/educational-resources/watergate/watergate-break.

"1:47 AM Found tape": DeNeen L. Brown. "'The Post' and the Forgotten Security Guard Who Discovered the Watergate Break-In." *Washington Post,* December 22, 2017. https://www.washingtonpost.com/news/retropolis/wp/2017/12/22/the-post-and-the-forgotten-security-guard-who-discovered-the-watergate-break-in/.

But for more than two years: Daniel Bush. "The Complete Watergate Timeline (It Took Longer than You Realize)." PBS, May 30, 2017. https://www.pbs.org/newshour/politics/complete-watergate-timeline-took-longer-realize.

On August 1: Ibid.

In April of the next year: Ibid.

37 *Yet, in November 1973:* "Nixon: 'I Am Not a Crook.'" History.com, November 17, 1973. https://www.history.com/topics/us-presidents/nixon-i-am-not-a-crook-video.

Asserting executive privilege: Marisa Iati. "Inside the Supreme Court Ruling That Made Nixon Turn over His Watergate Tapes." *Washington Post,* October 3, 2019. https://www.washingtonpost.com/history/2019/10/03/inside-supreme-court-ruling-that-made-nixon-turn-over-his-watergate-tapes/.

Recognizing that he had no chance: Richard Nixon. "President Nixon's Resignation Speech," August 8, 1974. https://www.pbs.org/newshour/spc/character/links/nixon_speech.html.

38 *As President Trump's phone call:* Peter Baker. "'We Absolutely Could Not Do That': When Seeking Foreign Help Was Out of the Question." *New York Times,* October 6, 2019. https://www.nytimes.com/2019/10/06/us/politics/trump-foreign-influence.html.

James A. Baker III: Ibid.

39 *"most deadly adversaries":* Alexander Hamilton. *The Federalist Papers: No. 68,* 1788. https://avalon.law.yale.edu/18th_century/fed68.asp.

It led to the natural-born citizen clause: The Constitution of the United States of America, Article II, Section 1.

40 *It led to the emoluments clause:* The Constitution of the United States of America, Article I, Section 9.

As Edmund Randolph: Jonathan Elliot, *The Debates in Several State Conventions of the Adoption of the Federal Constitution,* 1827, p. 36.

Within years of the Constitution's: Jordan Taylor, "Perspective | The Founding Fathers Knew First-Hand That Foreign Interference in U.S. Elections Was Dangerous," *Washington Post,* October 7, 2019, https://www.washingtonpost.com/outlook/2019/10/07/founders-knew-first-hand-that-foreign-interference-us-elections-was-dangerous/.

"Throughout the 1790s": "The Citizen Genêt Affair, 1793–1794," United States Department of State Office of the Historian, accessed October 24, 2019, https://history.state.gov/milestones/1784-1800/citizen-genet.

Genêt's successors: Taylor, "The Founding Fathers Knew First-Hand That Foreign Interference in U.S. Elections Was Dangerous."

"One newspaper writer": Ibid.

2. The Evidence

42 *Early in the summer of 2019:* "Transcript: ABC News' George Stephanopoulos' Exclusive Interview with President Trump," *Good Morning America,* June 16, 2019, https://www.goodmorningamerica.com/news/story/transcript-abc-news-george-stephanopoulos-exclusive-interview-president-63749144.

43 *When President Trump's comments:* John Cassidy, "The Stephanopoulos Interview Is Another Fine Mess for Trump | The New Yorker," *The New Yorker,* June 15, 2019, https://www.newyorker.com/news/our-columnists/the-stephanopoulos-interview-is-another-fine-mess-for-trump.

Sean Hannity resorted: Erik Wemple, "Opinion | George Stephanopoulos Is Filleting President Trump, Clip by Clip," *Washington Post,* June 14, 2019, https://www.washingtonpost.com/opinions/2019/06/14/george-stephanopoulos-is-filleting-president-trump-clip-by-clip/.

Representative Tom Cole: Kyle Cheney and Rew Desiderio, "House Republicans Try to Spin Trump's Foreign Dirt Comment," *Politico,* accessed October 15, 2019, https://politi.co/2IfyKel.

Even Republican senator: "Graham on Foreign Influence on American Elections," United States Senator Lindsey Graham, June 13, 2019, https://www.lgraham.senate.gov/public/index.cfm/2019/6/graham-on-foreign-influence-on-american-elections.

A Trump Administration official: Matthew Choi, "'Let Me Make Something 100%

Clear': FEC Chair Lays down the Law on Foreign Help," *Politico*, accessed October 15, 2019, https://politi.co/2IErAiF.

As Cassidy wrote: Cassidy, "Fine Mess for Trump."

Even President Trump: Caitlin Oprysko, "Trump Goes on Fox to Clean up His Foreign Interference Comments," *Politico*, accessed October 15, 2019, https://politi co/2WKJzxR.

44 *In 2014, Russia annexed:* Caitlin Emma, and Connor O'Brien. "Trump Holds up Ukraine Military Aid Meant to Confront Russia." *Politico*, August 28, 2019. https://www.politico.com/story/2019/08/28/trump-ukraine-military-aid-russia-1689531.

In June of 2019: "Portman Announces Senate NDAA Authorizes $300 Million in Security Assistance for Ukraine | Senator Rob Portman," accessed October 15, 2019, https://www.portman.senate.gov/newsroom/portman-announces-senate-ndaa-authorizes-300-million-security-assistance-ukraine.

45 *Together, the State Department:* Gienger, "Timeline."

At the time: Ephrat Livni: "Trump's Ukraine Gambit Threatened US National Security," *Quartz*, accessed October 15, 2019, https://qz.com/1716182/trumps-ukraine-gambit-threatened-us-national-security/.

"Toward the end": Stefan Becket, Arden Farhi, Kathryn Watson, "Top diplomat tells lawmakers Ukraine aid was directly tied to investigations," CBS News, October 23, 2019

46 *In fact, Ambassador Taylor learned:* Ibid.

This account is corroborated: Charlie Savage and Josh Williams, "Read the Text Messages Between U.S. and Ukrainian Officials," *New York Times*, October 4, 2019, https://www.nytimes.com/interactive/2019/10/04/us/politics/ukraine-text-messages-volker.html.

As Ambassador Taylor noted: Ibid.

But after weeks of discussions: "Read Trump's phone conversation with Volodymyr Zelensky," *CNN Politics*, September 26, 2019. Accessed 10/23/2019, https://www.cnn.com/2019/09/25/politics/donald-trump-ukraine-transcript-call/index.html.

47 *The phone call took place on July 25:* Ibid.

But after a few civil exchanges: Ibid.

As Congressman Adam Schiff: "'A Classic Mafia-like Shakedown': Adam Schiff Reacts to Trump-Ukraine Call," *Axios*, accessed October 16, 2019, https://www.axios.com/adam-schiff-ukraine-trump-transcript-impeachment-0afa23fa-b4c9-4c87-ad67-456624df3f3a.html.

Over the course of mere seconds: "Read Trump's phone conversation with Volodymyr Zelensky," *CNN Politics*.

These shoulder-fired missile systems: Louis Martinez, "What Are Javelin Missiles and Why Did Trump Discuss Them with Ukraine's President?," *ABC News*, September 25, 2019, https://abcnews.go.com/Politics/javelin-missiles-ukraine/story?id=65855233.

48   *President Trump's response:* "Read Trump's phone conversation with Volodymyr Zelensky," *CNN Politics.*
This favor, it turned out: Ibid.
After a quick digression about the Russia investigation: Ibid.
Trump's claim on the call: Ibid.
Hunter and Joe Biden's activities: Gienger, "Timeline."

49   *As Republican senator Ron Johnson said:* Alex Ward, "2 Republican Senators Refute Trump's Ukraine-Biden Conspiracy Theory," *Vox,* October 7, 2019, https://www.vox.com/policy-and-politics/2019/10/7/20903398/trump-biden-ukraine-portman-johnson-impeachment.
Nevertheless, when Trump asked Zelensky: "Read Trump's phone conversation with Volodymyr Zelensky," *CNN Politics.*
Trump then confirmed that Attorney General William Barr: Ibid.
In response, Zelensky thanked Trump: Ibid.
This promise to launch an investigation: Ibid.

50   *This second quid pro quo:* Karoun Demirjian et al., "Officials' Texts Reveal Belief That Trump Wanted Probes as Condition of Ukraine Meeting," *Washington Post,* October 4, 2019, https://www.washingtonpost.com/world/national-security/this-is-when-the-inquiry-gets-real-former-us-special-envoy-to-ukraine-testifies-in-impeachment-probe-today/2019/10/03/51365c1b-5a01-4e44-872a-299b67949a5e_story.html.
"I look forward to seeing you in Washington": "Read Trump's phone conversation with Volodymyr Zelensky," *CNN Politics.*
Why, then, did President Zelensky: Karoun Demirjian et al., "Officials' Texts Reveal Belief That Trump Wanted Probes as Condition of Ukraine Meeting."

51   *The day after the phone call:* Whistleblower Complaint, 4.
But whatever action: Gienger, "Timeline."
After all, Congress had already appropriated: Caitlin Emma and Connor O'Brien, "Trump Holds up Ukraine Military Aid Meant to Confront Russia — POLITICO."
Over the course of the next week: Charlie Savage: "Text Messages Between U.S. and Ukrainian Officials."
In fact, according to Taylor's: Stefan Becket, Arden Farhi, Kathryn Watson, "Top diplomat tells lawmakers Ukraine aid was directly tied to investigations," *CBS News,* October 23, 2019, https://www.cbsnews.com/news/bill-taylor-opening-statement-read-the-full-text-of-the-top-us-diplomats-statement-to-congress/.

52   *"Everything," Taylor explained:* Stefan Becket, Arden Farhi, Kathryn Watson, "Top diplomat tells lawmakers Ukraine aid was directly tied to investigations," CBS News, October 23, 2019, https://www.cbsnews.com/news/bill-taylor-opening-statement-read-the-full-text-of-the-top-us-diplomats-statement-to-congress/https://www.cbsnews.com/news/bill-taylor-opening-statement-read-the-full-text-of-the-top-us-diplomats-statement-to-congress/.
More than two months: Charlie Savage, "Text Messages Between U.S. and Ukrainian Officials."

When Taylor sent that message: Rebecca Ballhaus and Byron Tau, "Gordon Sond-land to Testify He Took Trump's Denial of Ukraine Quid Pro Quo at His Word — WSJ," October 13, 2019, https://www.wsj.com/articles/sondland-to-testify-he-took-trumps-denial-of-ukraine-quid-pro-quo-at-his-word-11570933206.

September 9, 2019, Text Messages: "Gordon Sondland Texts," *House of Repre-sentatives,* accessed October 17, 2019, https://www.documentcloud.org/docu ments/6451371-Volker-docs.html.

53 *Sondland had been a hotelier:* Deirdre Shesgreen, "Impeachment: Gordon Sond-land, Donor-Turned-Diplomat, a Central Player in Ukraine Controversy," *USA Today,* accessed October 16, 2019, https://www.usatoday.com/story/news/ politics/2019/10/08/who-gordon-sondland-trump-ambassador-to-eu-im peachment-witness-key-player-ukraine/3867905002/.

54 *Moreover, according to the:* Nicholas Fandos and Adam Goldman, "Ex-Aide Saw Gordon Sondland as a Potential National Security Risk," *New York Times,* Oc-tober 16, 2019, https://www.nytimes.com/2019/10/16/us/politics/gordon-sond land-intelligence-risk.html; Stefan Becket, Arden Farhi, Kathryn Watson, "Top diplomat tells lawmakers Ukraine aid was directly tied to investigations," CBS News, October 23, 2019, https://www.cbsnews.com/news/bill-taylor-opening-statement-read-the-full-text-of-the-top-us-diplomats-statement-to-congress/.

No wonder national security adviser: Peter Baker and Nicholas Fandos, "Bolton Objected to Ukraine Pressure Campaign, Calling Giuliani 'a Hand Grenade,'" *New York Times,* October 14, 2019, https://www.nytimes.com/2019/10/14/us/politics/ bolton-giuliani-fiona-hill-testimony.html.

One month earlier: Gienger, "Timeline."

55 *On August 12, 2019:* Viola Gienger and Ryan Goodman, "Timeline: Trump, Gi-uliani, and Ukrainegate (Updated)," Just Security, September 24, 2019, https:// www.justsecurity.org/66271/timeline-trump-giuliani-bidens-and-ukrainegate/.

The inspector general: Natasha Bertrand and Daniel Lippman, "The Intelligence Watchdog at the Center of the Ukraine Firestorm," Politico, September 23, 2019, https://www.politico.com/story/2019/09/23/atkinson-trump-ukraine-whistleblower-scandal-1508594.

But after IG Atkinson: Gienger, "Timeline."

Yet weeks went by: Mary Clare Jalonick, "A Look at Controversy over Intelligence Whistleblower Law," Associated Press, September 20, 2019, https://www.apnews. com/cffbe8af1d8440ee9c3b7f3ce37c19e8.

56 *Just seven months after:* Christopher Klein, "The United States Began Protecting Whistleblowers in 1777," HISTORY, accessed October 16, 2019, https://www.his tory.com/news/whistleblowers-law-founding-fathers.

That law came about as a result: Ibid.

But the whistleblowers eventually: Stephen M. Kohn, "The Whistle-Blowers of 1777," The New York Times, June 12, 2011, https://www.whistleblowers.org/wp-content/uploads/2018/11/1777whistle-blowers.pdf.

57 *Ever since, America hasn't only protected:* A. Ernest Fitzgerald, once called 'Amer-

ica's most famous whistleblower,' dies at 92," National Whistleblower Center, February 8, 2019, https://www.whistleblowersblog.org/2019/02/articles/whistleblower-news/a-ernest-fitzgerald-once-americas-most-famous-whistleblower-dies-at-92/; "Robert MacLean, Air Marshal Whistleblower," Government Accountability Project, accessed October 14, 2019, https://www.whistleblower.org/robert-maclean-air-marshal-whistleblower/.

The MacLean case is the last time: Brief of Members of Congress as Amici Curiae in Support of Respondent, Department of Homeland Security v. MacLean, 7, http://sblog.s3.amazonaws.com/wp-content/uploads/2014/11/13-894-bsac-Members-of-Congress.pdf.

One reason Congress appreciates: "Intelligence Community Whistleblower Protections," Congressional Research Service, 3, https://fas.org/sgp/crs/intel/R45345.pdf.

58   *in the days after the news:* Greg Miller, Ellen Nakashima, and Shane Harris, "Trump's Communications with Foreign Leader Are Part of Whistleblower Complaint that Spurred Standoff Between Spy Chief and Congress, Former Officials Say," *Washington Post,* September 18, 2019, https://www.washingtonpost.com/national-security/trumps-communications-with-foreign-leader-are-part-of-whistleblower-complaint-that-spurred-standoff-between-spy-chief-and-congress-former-officials-say/2019/09/18/df651aa2-da60-11e9-bfb1-849887369476_story.html.

That was when CNN host: "Chris Cuomo Clashes with Joe Biden Over Ukraine," filmed September 19, 2019, Washington, DC, video, https://www.youtube.com/watch?v=q6EHQKL2wdo.

59   *Giuliani's interview:* Zachary Cohen et al., "Trump Pushed Ukraine to Investigate Joe Biden, Transcript Shows," CNNPolitics, September 25, 2019, https://www.cnn.com/2019/09/25/politics/donald-trump-ukraine-transcript/index.html.

With every hour: Matt Zapotosky and Devlin Barrett, "Trump Administration Again Pushes Limits of Authority in Shielding Whistleblower Complaint from Congress," *Washington Post,* September 23, 2019, https://www.washingtonpost.com/national-security/trump-administration-again-pushes-limits-of-authority-in-shielding-whistleblower-complaint-from-congress/2019/09/23/734603ee-de35-11e9-8dc8-498eabc129a0_story.html.

So on September 24: Gienger, "Timeline."

And House Speaker Nancy Pelosi decided: Marina Pitofsky, "READ: Speaker Pelosi Announces Impeachment Inquiry," The Hill, September 24, 2019, https://thehill.com/blogs/blog-briefing-room/uncategorized/462889-read-speaker-pelosi-announces-impeachment-inquiry.

The following morning: Gienger, "Timeline."

60   *The morning IG Atkinson:* Ben Rhodes, "Ben Rhodes on Twitter: 'So the Barr DoJ Was Suppressing a Whistle Blower Complaint That Apparently Implicates Barr in Trump's Ukraine Scheme. The Corruption Is Everywhere in This Administra-

tion.' / Twitter," Twitter, accessed October 16, 2019, https://twitter.com/brhodes/
status/1176887571428909056.

Notably, this Legal Counsell: Council of the Inspectors General, Letter to Steven
A. Engel, Oct. 22, 2019, https://www.documentcloud.org/documents/6523365-
CIGIE-Letter-to-OLC-Whistleblower-Disclosure.html.

This ruling from the DOJ: Kathryn Watson, "What to Know about the Mysteri-
ous Whistleblower Complaint Involving Trump," *CBS News*, September 19, 2019,
https://www.cbsnews.com/news/whistleblower-complaint-what-to-know-about-
the-report-to-the-dni-involving-trump-being-kept-from-congress/.

But later that morning: Li Zhou, "Even Senate Republicans Want to See a Whistleblower Report on Trump," *Vox,* September 24, 2019, https://www.vox.com/
policy-and-politics/2019/9/24/20882420/mitch-mconnell-chuck-schumer-
senate-resolution-whistleblower-report.

61   *In the course of my official duties:* Whistleblower Complaint.

62   *When President Trump:* Ibid.
      These White House officials: Ibid.
      "White House officials told me": Ibid.

63   *The only apparent reason President Trump's lawyers:* Ibid.
      In his appendix: Ibid., appx. 1.
      The whistleblower did not specify: Pamela Brown, Jim Sciutto, and Kevin Liptak,
      "White House Restricted Access to Trump's Calls with Putin and Saudi Crown
      Prince — CNNPolitics," *CNN Politics,* accessed October 16, 2019, https://www.
      cnn.com/2019/09/27/politics/white-house-restricted-trump-calls-putin-saudi/
      index.html.

64   *The whistleblower's complaint:* Whistleblower Complaint, 4.
      The story began: Ibid.
      Ukrainian officials, Lutsenko claimed: Gienger, "Timeline."
      President Trump's own State Department: Ibid.
      "I went to his office": Tracy Wilkinson and Sergei Loiko, "Former Ukraine Pros-
      ecutor Says He Saw No Evidence of Wrongdoing by Biden," *Los Angeles Times,*
      September 29, 2019, https://www.latimes.com/politics/story/2019-09-29/
      former-ukraine-prosecutor-says-no-wrongdoing-biden.

65   *When I talked to:* Camilo Montoya-Galvez, "Giuliani Says Pompeo Told Him He
      Was Aware of Ukraine Outreach," September 29, 2019, https://www.cbsnews.
      com/news/rudy-giuliani-on-face-the-nation-says-mike-pompeo-told-him-he-
      was-aware-of-ukraine-outreach/.
      Secretary of Energy Rick Perry: Timothy Puko and Rebecca Ballhaus, "Rick Perry
      Called Rudy Giuliani at Trump's Direction on Ukraine Concerns," *Wall Street
      Journal,* October 16, 2019, https://www.wsj.com/articles/rick-perry-called-
      rudy-giuliani-at-trumps-direction-on-ukraine-concerns-11571273635.
      Even Ambassador Sondland told Congress: Josh Lederman. "Sondland to Testify
      That Trump Directed Giuliani to Push Ukraine Scheme." *NBC News,* October

17, 2019. https://www.nbcnews.com/politics/trump-impeachment-inquiry/sond land-testify-trump-directed-giuliani-push-ukraine-scheme-n1067986.

So perhaps it's no surprise that: Gregg Re, "Clinton-Ukraine Collusion Allegations 'big' and 'Incredible,' Will Be Reviewed, Trump Says," *Fox News,* April 25, 2019, https://www.foxnews.com/politics/trump-barr-will-look-at-incredible-possibility-of-ukraine-clinton-collusion.

Four days after that television appearance: "Read Marie Yovanovitch's Prepared Deposition Statement," *Washington Post,* October 11, 2019, https://www.wash ingtonpost.com/context/read-marie-yovanovitch-s-prepared-deposition-state ment/dffbf543-a373-46e0-a957-bc12a9371af4/.

Although I understand: Ibid.

When Giuliani was asked: Whistleblower Complaint, p. 6.

About 72 hours after: Ibid.

66   *This might seem like a spectacular allegation:* Kenneth P. Vogel. "Rudy Giuliani Plans Ukraine Trip to Push for Inquiries That Could Help Trump," May 9, 2019. https://www.nytimes.com/2019/05/09/us/politics/giuliani-ukraine-trump.html.

But with the spotlight on him: Gienger, "Timeline."

Around this time: Whistleblower Complaint, p. 7.

These efforts: Ibid.

By mid-May: Paul Farhi. "How a Conservative Columnist Helped Push a Flawed Ukraine Narrative." *Washington Post,* September 29, 2019. https://www.wash ingtonpost.com/lifestyle/style/how-a-conservative-columnist-helped-push-a-flawed-ukraine-narrative/2019/09/26/1654026e-dee7-11e9-8dc8-498eabc129a0_ story.html.

67   *"Shortly after President Zelensky's inauguration":* Whistleblower Complaint, p. 7.

As two of his aides: Evan Perez, Michael Warren, and David Shortell, "Two Men Connected to Giuliani's Ukraine Efforts Charged with Funneling Foreign Money into US Election — CNNPolitics," October 10, 2019, https://www.cnn. com/2019/10/10/politics/guliani-client-arrested-campaign-finance/index.html.

"On 13 June": Whistleblower Complaint, p. 7.

68   *"The reality is the president":* Tim Hains, "Giuliani: Trump Has Every Right To Ask Other Countries For Help With Criminal Investigations; What If Biden Had Killed Someone?," *RealClear Politics* October 6, 2019, https://www. realclearpolitics.com/video/2019/10/06/giuliani_trump_has_every_right_to_ ask_other_countries_for_help_with_criminal_investigations_what_if_biden_ killed_someone.html.

The following day: Aaron Blake, "Analysis | Trump Just Inched toward Spilling the Beans on Ukraine," *Washington Post,* September 23, 2019, https://www.washing-tonpost.com/politics/2019/09/23/trump-inches-toward-spilling-beans-ukraine/.

CNBC reporter: Aaron Rupar, "Trump Insists He Just Wants Foreign Countries to Tackle 'Corruption.' Here's Why That's Absurd.," *Vox,* October 4, 2019, https://www.vox.com/2019/10/4/20899087/trump-corruption-investigation-ukraine-china-scandal.

69 *"When the only American citizen"*: "Mitt Romney on Twitter: 'When the Only American Citizen President Trump Singles out for China's Investigation Is His Political Opponent in the Midst of the Democratic Nomination Process, It Strains Credulity to Suggest That It Is Anything Other than Politically Motivated.' / Twitter," Twitter, October 4, 2019, https://twitter.com/mittromney/status/1180151212030779392.

Making matters worse: Samantha Vinograd, "This Is What a Legitimate Anti-Corruption Effort in Ukraine Would Look Like — POLITICO Magazine," *Politico*, October 9, 2019, https://www.politico.com/magazine/story/2019/10/09/donald-trump-impeachment-ukraine-corruption-rudy-giuliani-joe-biden-229828.

an official letter to Congress: John Rood, "Pentagon Letter on Ukraine Aid," NPR News, May, 2019, https://apps.npr.org/documents/document.html?id=6430088-Pentagon-Letter-On-Ukraine-Aid.

70 *"I'll continue to withhold [the funding]"*: Betsy Klein, "Trump Admits He Delayed Ukraine Aid but Claims It Was Unrelated to Biden," CNN, September 24, 2019, https://www.cnn.com/2019/09/24/politics/donald-trump-ukraine-aid/index.html.

71 *As Senator Lindsey Graham tweeted*: "Lindsey Graham on Twitter: 'In America You Can't Even Get a Parking Ticket Based on Hearsay Testimony. But You Can Impeach a President? I Certainly Hope Not.' / Twitter," Twitter, accessed October 17, 2019, https://twitter.com/lindseygrahamsc/status/1177941037895036928.

Two days later: "Donald J. Trump on Twitter: 'So If the so-Called "Whistleblower" Has All Second Hand Information, and Almost Everything He Has Said about My "Perfect" Call with the Ukrainian President Is Wrong (Much to the Embarrassment of Pelosi & Schiff), Why Aren't We Entitled to Interview & Learn Everything about . . .' / Twitter," Twitter, accessed October 17, 2019, https://twitter.com/realdonaldtrump/status/1179023001989373952.

In audio from a private event: Eli Stokols, "Listen: Audio of Trump Discussing Whistleblower at Private Event: 'That's Close to a Spy' — Los Angeles Times," *Los Angeles Times*, September 26, 2019, https://www.latimes.com/politics/story/2019-09-26/trump-at-private-breakfast-who-gave-the-whistle-blower-the-information-because-thats-almost-a-spy.

The way "we" used to "handle": Ryan Bort, "Oh, Nothing, Just Trump Fantasizing About Executing 'Spies' Behind the Whistle-Blower Complaint," *Rolling Stone*, September 26, 2019, https://www.rollingstone.com/politics/politics-news/oh-nothing-just-trump-fantasizing-about-executing-spies-behind-the-whistle-blower-complaint-891093/.

72 *"I have an absolute right"*: "Donald J. Trump on Twitter: 'As the President of the United States, I Have an Absolute Right, Perhaps Even a Duty, to Investigate, or Have Investigated, CORRUPTION, and That Would Include Asking, or Suggesting, Other Countries to Help Us out!' / Twitter," Twitter, October 3, 2019, https://twitter.com/realdonaldtrump/status/1179925259417468928.

Trump brought this message: Kevin Breuninger, "Trump Says China Should Investigate the Bidens, Doubles down on Ukraine Probe," CNBC, October 3, 2019, https://www.cnbc.com/2019/10/03/trump-calls-for-ukraine-china-to-investigate-the-bidens.html.

Acting chief of staff: Savannah Behrmann, "'Get Over It': Trump campaign sells T-shirts following Mulvaney quid pro quo comments," *USA Today,* October 18, 2019, https://www.usatoday.com/story/news/politics/elections/2019/10/18/get-over-it-trump-campaign-sells-t-shirts-mulvaney/4025702002/.

73   *When Speaker Pelosi opened:* Allan Smith and Geoff Bennett, "State Department Blocks Ambassador from Testifying in Trump Impeachment Inquiry," *NBC News,* accessed October 17, 2019, https://www.nbcnews.com/politics/donald-trump/trump-administration-orders-ambassador-center-ukraine-scandal-not-appear-congress-n1063636.

"In order to fulfill his duties": Ella Nilsen, "Read: The White House Letter Refusing to Comply with Democrats' Impeachment Inquiry," *Vox,* October 8, 2019, https://www.vox.com/policy-and-politics/2019/10/8/20905469/white-house-letter-democrats-impeachment-inquiry.

Executive privilege: Ibid.

3. The Case Against President Trump

75   *As Alexander Hamilton wrote:* Alexander Hamilton, *The Federalist Papers: No. 65.*

78   *As you may recall:* Julian Borger. "Mike Flynn at Risk of Russian Blackmail, Sally Yates Warned White House." *The Guardian,* May 8, 2017. https://www.theguardian.com/us-news/2017/may/08/sally-yates-trump-russia-michael-flynn-blackmail-compromised.

79   *At a news conference:* Michael S. Schmidt. "Trump Invited the Russians to Hack Clinton. Were They Listening?" *New York Times,* July 13, 2018. https://www.nytimes.com/2018/07/13/us/politics/trump-russia-clinton-emails.html.

before long John Podesta: Aaron Sharockman. "It's True: WikiLeaks Dumped Podesta Emails Hour after Trump Video Surfaced." *PolitiFact* (blog), December 18, 2016. https://www.politifact.com/truth-o-meter/statements/2016/dec/18/john-podesta/its-true-wikileaks-dumped-podesta-emails-hour-afte/.

80   *In all, Mueller's report delineated:* The Editorial Board. "The Mueller Report and the Danger Facing American Democracy." *New York Times,* April 19, 2019. https://www.nytimes.com/2019/04/19/opinion/mueller-report-trump-russia.html.

These included a meeting: Allan Smith, "Mueller Declined to Charge Donald Trump Jr. for Meeting with Russian Lawyer," *NBC News,* April 18, 2019, https://www.nbcnews.com/politics/donald-trump/mueller-report-no-evidence-trump-knew-about-trump-tower-meeting-n995816.

Regardless of what information: Robert Mueller III. "Report On The Investigation Into Russian Interference In The 2016 Presidential Election." United States Department of Justice, 2019, 13. https://www.justice.gov/storage/report.pdf.

81   *What's worse:* Associated Press. "Mueller Cites 'efforts' to Meddle in Election."
      PBS, May 20, 2019. https://www.pbs.org/newshour/politics/mueller-cites-
      efforts-to-meddle-in-election.

      Russia's interference in 2016: Cynthia McFadden, William M. Arkin, and Kevin
      Monahan. "Russians Penetrated U.S. Voter Systems, Top U.S. Official Says." NBC
      News, February 7, 2018. https://www.nbcnews.com/politics/elections/russians-
      penetrated-u-s-voter-systems-says-top-u-s-n845721.

      In fact, according to the Washington Post: Shane Harris, Josh Dawsey, and El-
      len Nakashima. "Trump Told Russian Officials in 2017 He Wasn't Concerned
      about Moscow's Interference in U.S. Election." *Washington Post,* September
      27, 2019. https://www.washingtonpost.com/national-security/trump-told-rus
      sian-officials-in-2017-he-wasnt-concerned-about-moscows-interference-in-us-
      election/2019/09/27/b20a8bc8-e159-11e9-b199-f638bf2c340f_story.html.

82   *As Gouverneur Morris:* "Madison Debates," Ibid.

83   *For this reason:* Laurence Tribe and Joshua Matz, *To End a Presidency: The Power
      of Impeachment,* 33.

      As far as the founders were concerned: Ben Berwick, Justin Florence, and John
      Langford. "The Constitution Says 'Bribery' Is Impeachable. What Does That
      Mean?" *Lawfare* (blog), October 3, 2019. https://www.lawfareblog.com/constitu
      tion-says-bribery-impeachable-what-does-mean.

84   *In the weeks after news broke:* Bribery of public officials and witnesses, § 201(b)(1).
      https://www.law.cornell.edu/uscode/text/18/201.

      Indeed, the mayor of Detroit: Ed White. "Former Detroit Mayor Sentenced to 28
      Years for 'pay-to-Play' Bribery." *NBC News,* October 11, 2013. https://www.nbc
      news.com/news/us-news/former-detroit-mayor-sentenced-28-years-pay-play-
      bribery-flna8C11368978.

      The first came: "Full Document: Trump's Call With the Ukrainian President,"
      New York Times, September 25, 2019, sec. US, https://www.nytimes.com/inter
      active/2019/09/25/us/politics/trump-ukraine-transcript.html.

85   *That's why House leader Kevin McCarthy:* Scott Pelley. The Impeachment In-
      quiry: Nancy Pelosi, Kevin McCarthy, and Adam Schiff. *60 Minutes,* Septem-
      ber 30, 2019. https://www.cbsnews.com/news/nancy-pelosi-on-trump-impeac
      hment-inquiry-ukraine-president-phone-call-and-the-whistleblower-in-60-
      minutes-interview/.

      Ross Spano: Veronica Stracqualursi. "Quid pro Quo: What It Means." *CNN Politics,*
      September 27, 2019. https://www.cnn.com/2019/09/26/politics/quid-pro-quo-
      trump-ukraine-call/index.html.

      And in a text exchange: Karoun Demirjian, Rachael Bade, Josh Dawsey, and
      John Hudson. "Officials' Texts Reveal Belief That Trump Wanted Probes as
      Condition of Ukraine Meeting." *Washington Post,* October 4, 2019. https://
      www.washingtonpost.com/world/national-security/this-is-when-the-inquiry-
      gets-real-former-us-special-envoy-to-ukraine-testifies-in-impeachment-probe-
      today/2019/10/03/51365c1b-5a01-4e44-872a-299b67949a5e_story.html.

On the call itself: "Read Trump's phone conversation with Volodymyr Zelensky," *CNN Politics.*

87 *In his conduct of the office:* "Articles of Impeachment Against President Richard Nixon." House Judiciary Committee, July 27, 1974.

88 *In all, Article I:* Ibid.

Alexander Butterfield didn't have anything to do: Alicia Shepard, "The Man Who Revealed the Nixon Tapes," *Washington Post,* June 14, 2012, https://www.washingtonpost.com/opinions/the-man-who-revealed-the-nixon-tapes/2012/06/14/gJQAsEZUdV_story.html.

"I was sort of surprised": Ibid.

89 *When he was finally asked if he would speak:* Ibid.

But when Butterfield: Ibid.

Alexander Butterfield was no willing: Ibid.

"The President would personally listen": Bob Woodward and Carl Bernstein, *The Final Days* (Simon & Schuster, 1976), p. 62.

90 *The president's advisers ultimately deemed:* Ibid., p. 63.

When Cox: Ibid., pp. 68–72.

But once investigators: Nixon Articles of Impeachment.

91 *In Article III:* Ibid.

To quote Senator Lindsey Graham: Ryan Bort, "Impeachment Inquiry: Lindsey Graham Argued for Congressional Oversight."

the whistleblower details an operation: Whistleblower Complaint, p. 3.

92 *Once members:* King et al., "Acting DNI Defends His Role In Handling Of Whistleblower Complaint."

The stated reason for doing so: Ibid.

The Justice Department joined: Alexander Mallin, "Trump's DOJ Clears President of Violating Campaign Finance Law in Ukraine-Biden Call — ABC News," *ABC News,* September 25, 2019, https://preview.abcnews.go.com/Politics/trumps-doj-clears-president-violating-campaign-finance-law/story?id=65849857.

This decision didn't make any sense: Zoe Tillman, "The Justice Department Has Argued Sex, Information, And Worthless Stock Were 'Things Of Value.' But It Said Trump's Request For Dirt Wasn't," *BuzzFeed News,* October 3, 2019, https://www.buzzfeednews.com/article/zoetillman/justice-department-trump-call-ukraine-thing-value.

Moreover, a longstanding: Neal Katyal and Joshua Geltzer, "Opinion | Was There Another Cover-Up In Response to the Whistle-Blower?," *New York Times,* October 2, 2019, https://www.nytimes.com/2019/10/02/opinion/trump-whistleblower-fec.html.

93 *Trump has claimed:* David A. Graham, "The Mystery of the Ukraine-Call Transcript," *Atlantic,* October 4, 2019, https://www.theatlantic.com/ideas/archive/2019/10/do-we-actually-know-what-happened-zelensky-call/599359/.

There are also three sets of ellipses: Carol D. Leonnig, Craig Timberg, and Drew

Harwell, "Odd Markings, Ellipses Fuel Doubts about the Rough Transcript of Trump's Ukraine Call," *Washington Post*, October 2, 2019, https://www.washingtonpost.com/technology/2019/10/03/odd-markings-ellipses-fuel-doubts-about-rough-transcript-trumps-ukraine-call/.

94   *Even before President Trump's:* Neal Katyal. "Trump's Abuse of Executive Privilege Is More Than a Present Danger." *New York Times*, July 17, 2019. https://www.nytimes.com/2019/06/17/opinion/trump-executive-privilege.html.

95   *"In defending Trump":* David A. Graham, "Trump's Defeat on Tax Returns Signals a Big Problem for the President," *Atlantic*, October 7, 2019, https://www.theatlantic.com/ideas/archive/2019/10/marrero-ruling-trump-cy-vance-immunity/599536/.

     On indictment: Renae Reints. "Why Couldn't Mueller Indict Trump? This DOJ Policy Prevented Him." *Fortune*, May 30, 2019. https://fortune.com/2019/05/30/indict-a-sitting-president-doj-policy/.

96   *Nixon differentiated himself from his predecessors:* Marc Fisher, "'He Ignores the Law When He Doesn't like It,'" *Washington Post*, September 23, 2019, https://www.washingtonpost.com/politics/when-the-president-does-it-that-means-its-not-illegal/2019/09/22/62559ea6-dcb8-11e9-ac63-3016711543fe_story.html.

97   *In the wake of Nixon's resignation:* Neal Katyal, "Opinion | Trump's Abuse of Executive Privilege Is More Than a Present Danger," *New York Times*, June 17, 2019, https://www.nytimes.com/2019/06/17/opinion/trump-executive-privilege.html.

     The exception: Assertations of Executive Privilege from Kennedy to Obama, Reporters Committee for the Freedom of the Press, https://www.rcfp.org/journals/assertions-executive-privileg/.

     Clinton's use of executive privilege: Katyal, "Opinion | Trump's Abuse of Executive Privilege Is More Than a Present Danger."

98   *Shortly thereafter, President Trump tweeted:* "Donald J. Trump on Twitter: 'I Would Love to Send Ambassador Sondland, a Really Good Man and Great American, to Testify, but Unfortunately He Would Be Testifying before a Totally Compromised Kangaroo Court, Where Republican's Rights Have Been Taken Away, and True Facts Are Not Allowed out for the Public . . . ,'" Twitter, October 8, 2019, https://twitter.com/realdonaldtrump/status/1181560708808486914.

     That same day: "Letter from White House Counsel Pat Cipollone to House leaders," *Washington Post*, October 8, 2019.

     Cipollone's eight-page letter: David A. Graham, "Trump's Obstruction Letter," *The Atlantic*, October 9, 2019, https://www.theatlantic.com/ideas/archive/2019/10/trump-letter-promises-complete-obstruction/599689/.

99   *On the other hand:* Andrew Desiderio, and Kyle Cheney. "House Lawyers: Trump Trying to 'Obstruct His Own Impeachment.'" *Politico*, October 16, 2019. https://www.politico.com/news/2019/10/16/trump-impeachment-house-obstruction-049394.

     Indeed, they recently: Spencer S. Hsu. "U.S. Judge Balks at Justice Dept. Bid to

Deny House Access to Mueller Grand Jury Materials." *Washington Post*, October 8, 2019. https://www.washingtonpost.com/local/legal-issues/us-judge-balks-at-justice-dept-bid-to-deny-house-access-to-mueller-grand-jury-materials/2019/10/08/bd0de590-e9c6-11e9-9c6d-436a0df4f31d_story.html.

100 *While none of Special Counsel Mueller's findings:* Robert S. Mueller III, "Report on the Investigation into Russian Interference in the 2016 Presidential Election," March 2019, https://www.documentcloud.org/documents/5955118-The-Mueller-Report.html.

101 *by claiming Adam Schiff:* Isaac Stanley-Becker, "Trump says 'treason.' His fans invoke violence. How attacks against Schiff are escalating online," *Washington Post*, October 14, 2019, https://www.washingtonpost.com/politics/trump-says-treason-his-fans-invoke-violence-how-attacks-against-schiff-are-escalating-online/2019/10/14/9f613974-ec4c-11e9-9306-47cb0324fd44_story.html.

by calling the impeachment probe a "coup": David A. Graham, "Trump's Defeat on Tax Returns Signals a Big Problem for the President," *The Atlantic*, October 7, 2019,

102 *As John Dean:* George T. Conway and Neal Katyal, "Trump has done plenty to warrant impeachment. But the Ukraine allegations are over the top," *Washington Post*, September 20, 2019, https://www.washingtonpost.com/politics/trump-says-treason-his-fans-invoke-violence-how-attacks-against-schiff-are-escalating-online/2019/10/14/9f613974-ec4c-11e9-9306-47cb0324fd44_story.html.

4. Questions and Answers

107 *How does impeachment actually work:* Charles L. Black and Philip Bobbitt, *Impeachment: A Handbook*.

After all, the procedures the Senate: Laurence Tribe and Joshua Matz, *To End a Presidency: The Power of Impeachment*.

108 *As law professor Charles Black wrote:* Charles L. Black and Philip Bobbitt, *Impeachment: A Handbook*, p. 14.

109 *To quote Senator Lindsey Graham:* Ryan Bort, "The Best Argument Against the White House Stonewalling Congress Was Made by . . . Lindsey Graham."

111 *The president cannot easily be compelled:* Andy Wright, "Can Congress Subpoena Trump to Testify?," Just Security, November 27, 2018, https://www.justsecurity.org/61535/congress-subpoena-trump-testify/.

113 *What does the Senate do?:* Charles L. Black and Philip Bobbitt, *Impeachment: A Handbook*.

As soon as the House votes: Ibid., p. 17.

As Chief Justice William Rehnquist: Joan Biskupic. "The Rehnquist Files: How the Last Chief Justice Handled an Impeachment Trial." CNN, September 29, 2019. https://www.cnn.com/2019/09/29/politics/william-rehnquist-impeachment-trial-senate/index.html.

114 *The rulebook reads:* "United States Senate Manual, 104th Congress-Rules of Procedure and Practice in the Senate when Sitting on Impeachment Trials," govinfo.

gov, accessed October 20, 2019, https://www.govinfo.gov/content/pkg/SMAN-104/html/SMAN-104-pg177.htm.

But Senator Mitch McConnell: Ron Elving, "What Happened With Merrick Garland In 2016 And Why It Matters Now," NPR, June 29, 2018, https://www.npr.org/2018/06/29/624467256/what-happened-with-merrick-garland-in-2016-and-why-it-matters-now.

The good news is: Marianne Levine, "McConnell: Senate Would Have 'No Choice' but to Take up Impeachment," *Politico,* September 30, 2019, https://politi.co/2n-RiCIi.

115   *As McConnell wrote in a fundraising pitch:* Anna Kaplan, "Mitch McConnell in Campaign Ad: Impeachment Will Fail 'With Me As Majority Leader,'" *Daily Beast,* October 5, 2019, https://www.thedailybeast.com/mitch-mcconnell-in-campaign-ad-impeachment-will-fail-with-me-as-majority-leader.

116   *As law professor Charles Black argues:* Charles L. Black and Philip Bobbitt, *Impeachment: A Handbook,* p. 17.

There are no requirements: "Impeachment Time Line — Andrew Johnson," US National Park Service, accessed October 20, 2019, https://www.nps.gov/anjo/learn/historyculture/impeachmenttimeline.htm; Jon Meacham et al., *Impeachment: An American History;* "A Timeline of How the Clinton Impeachment Went Down," CNN, September 25, 2019, https://www.cnn.com/politics/live-news/trump-impeachment-inquiry-09-25-2019/h_f5b7df188bc47c1da03d9ea6f5503cef.

117   *Speaker Pelosi and congressional leadership:* Mike DeBonis and Rachel Bade: "Pelosi, top Democrats favor quick, narrow Trump impeachment probe focused on Ukraine," *Washington Post,* September 25, 2019, https://www.washingtonpost.com/powerpost/pelosi-privately-urges-narrow-trump-impeachment-probe-focused-on-ukraine/2019/09/25/c65b6f0c-dfab-11e9-be96-6adb81821e90_story.html.

The Supreme Court ruled: "Hearings Before the Senate Impeachment Trial Committee, United States Senate, One Hundred Eleventh Congress, Second Session, on the Articles of Impeachment Against Judge G. Thomas Porteous, Jr. a Judge in the United States District Court for the Eastern District of Louisiana," November 16, 2010.

This is in line with: Charles L. Black and Philip Bobbitt, *Impeachment: A Handbook,* p. 48.

That's another reason that the Supreme Court: "Hearings Before the Senate Impeachment Trial Committee, United States Senate, One Hundred Eleventh Congress, Second Session, on the Articles of Impeachment Against Judge G. Thomas Porteous, Jr. a Judge in the United States District Court for the Eastern District of Louisiana," November 16, 2010.

119   *To quote Vice President Mike Pence:* Ari Melber. "Mike Pence Address to Congress on Impeachment."

As I wrote in Chapter 2: Christopher Klein, "The United States Began Protecting Whistleblowers in 1777," *History,* accessed October 16, 2019, https://www. history.com/news/whistleblowers-law-founding-fathers.

120 *"whistleblowers play a vital":* Brief of Members of Congress as Amici Curiae in Support of Respondent, Department of Homeland Security v. MacLean, 7, http:// sblog.s3.amazonaws.com/wp-content/uploads/2014/11/13-894-bsac-Members-of-Congress.pdf.

President Obama and Congress: Michael E DeVine, "Intelligence Community Whistleblower Protections" (Congressional Research Service, September 23, 2019), https://fas.org/sgp/crs/intel/R45345.pdf.

By contrast, President Trump: Shannon Pettypiece, "Trump Says Those Who Gave Info to the Whistleblower Are like Spies, Reports Say," *NBC News,* September 26, 2019, https://www.nbcnews.com/politics/white-house/trump-says-our-country-stake-whistleblower-account-made-public-n1059011.

Whistleblowing is designed: Charlie Savage, "How the Law Protects Intelligence Whistle-Blowers, and Leaves Them at Risk," *New York Times,* October 3, 2019, https://www.nytimes.com/2019/10/03/us/politics/whistleblower-complaint.html.

In fact, the director of national intelligence: Noel King and Greg Myre, "Acting DNI Defends His Role In Handling Of Whistleblower Complaint," NPR, September 26, 2019, https://www.npr.org/2019/09/26/764645909/acting-dni-defends-his-role-in-handling-of-whistleblower-complaint.

121 *This whistleblower, in particular:* Natasha Bertrand, "Trump's Attacks Fuel Alarm That Whistleblower Protections Fall Short — POLITICO," *Politico,* October 9, 2019, https://www.politico.com/news/2019/10/09/trump-ukraine-whistleblower-attacks-043567; Pettypiece, "Trump Says Those Who Gave Info to the Whistleblower Are like Spies, Reports Say."

In fact, the Department: United States Department of Justice. A Sitting President's Amenability to Indictment and Criminal Protection (2000). https://www.justice.gov/file/19351/download.

122 *Trump seems to be:* Dara Lind: "Michael Cohen: 'Individual #1 is Donald J. Trump,'" *Vox,* February 27, 2019, https://www.vox.com/2019/2/27/18243038/individual-1-cohen-trump-mueller.

124 *At first, Gouverneur Morris:* "Madison Debates."

But Morris's point: Ibid.

125 *To quote the minutes:* Ibid.

126 *As Tribe and Matz write:* Laurence Tribe and Joshua Matz, *To End a Presidency: The Power of Impeachment.*

127 *Take, for example:* Article I, Nixon Articles of Impeachment.

128 *The first came:* "Read Trump's phone conversation with Volodymyr Zelensky," *CNN Politics.*

129 *The second quid pro quo:* Savage, et al., "Read the Text Messages Between U.S. and Ukrainian Officials."

On the call itself: "Read Trump's phone conversation with Volodymyr Zelensky," *CNN Politics.*

But don't just take it from me: Savage, et al., "Read the Text Messages Between U.S. and Ukrainian Officials."

And acting White House chief of staff: Blake, "Analysis | Trump's Acting Chief of Staff Admits It: There Was a Ukraine Quid pro Quo."

Taylor wasn't the only one: Greg Miller and Greg Jaffe, "At Least Four National Security Officials Raised Alarms about Ukraine Policy before and after Trump Call with Ukrainian President," *Washington Post,* October 10, 2019, https://www.washingtonpost.com/national-security/at-least-four-national-security-officials-raised-alarms-about-ukraine-policy-before-and-after-trump-call-with-ukrainian-president/2019/10/10/ffe0c88a-eb6d-11e9-9c6d-436a0df4f31d_story.html; Whistleblower Complaint.

131 *Lindsey Graham, in a tweet:* Lindsey Graham on Twitter: "In America You Can't Even Get a Parking Ticket Based on Hearsay Testimony. But You Can Impeach a President? I Certainly Hope Not."

132 *By all appearances:* Daryna Krasnolutska, Kateryna Choursina, and Stephanie Baker. "Ukraine Prosecutor Says No Evidence of Wrongdoing by Bidens." *Bloomberg News,* May 16, 2019. https://www.bloomberg.com/news/articles/2019-05-16/ukraine-prosecutor-says-no-evidence-of-wrongdoing-by-bidens.

As to the accusation: John Haltiwanger. "A Ukraine Gas Company Tied to Joe Biden's Son Is at the Center of the Trump-Whistleblower Scandal." *Business Insider,* October 4, 2019. https://www.businessinsider.com/ukraine-gas-company-burisma-holdings-joe-bidens-son-hunter-explained-2019-9.

133 *"When the only American citizen":* "Mitt Romney on Twitter: 'When the Only American Citizen President Trump Singles out for China's Investigation Is His Political Opponent in the Midst of the Democratic Nomination Process, It Strains Credulity to Suggest That It Is Anything Other than Politically Motivated.' / Twitter," Twitter, October 4, 2019, https://twitter.com/mittromney/status/1180151212030779392.

when Trump was asked: Aaron Rupar, "Trump Insists He Just Wants Foreign Countries to Tackle 'Corruption.' Here's Why That's Absurd.," Vox, October 4, 2019, https://www.vox.com/2019/10/4/20899087/trump-corruption-investigation-ukraine-china-scandal.

President Trump's own administration: John Rood, "Pentagon Letter on Ukraine Aid," NPR News, May, 2019, https://apps.npr.org/documents/document.html?id=6430088-Pentagon-Letter-On-Ukraine-Aid.

134 *President Trump cut:* Samantha Vinograd, "This Is What a Legitimate Anti-Corruption Effort in Ukraine Would Look Like — POLITICO Magazine," *Politico,* October 9, 2019, https://www.politico.com/magazine/story/2019/10/09/donald-trump-impeachment-ukraine-corruption-rudy-giuliani-joe-biden-229828.

If President Trump really wanted: Stefan Becket, Arden Farhi, Kathryn Watson, "Top diplomat tells lawmakers Ukraine aid was directly tied to investigations," *CBS News,* October 23, 2019, https://www.cbsnews.com/news/bill-taylor-opening-statement-read-the-full-text-of-the-top-us-diplomats-statement-to-congress/.

135   *Charles Black writes:* Charles L. Black and Philip Bobbitt, *Impeachment: A Handbook,* p. 12.

She even went across the country: Laurence Tribe and Joshua Matz, *To End a Presidency: The Power of Impeachment.*

136   *In fact, as I mentioned in Chapter 2:* Baker. "We Absolutely Could Not Do That."

"*most deadly adversaries*": Alexander Hamilton. *The Federalist Papers: No. 68,* 1788. https://avalon.law.yale.edu/18th_century/fed68.asp.

137   *That's why our Constitution:* US. Constitution, Article II, Section 1, and Article I, Section 9.

As one of our founders: Trickey, "Inside the Founding Fathers' Debate over what Constituted an Impeachable Offense."

On October 21, 2019: Abbey Marshall, "Trump Claims He's the Victim of 'Phony Emoluments Clause,'" *Politico,* October 21, 2019, https://www.politico.com/news/2019/10/21/trump-emoluments-clause-053289.

Lawrence Hogan, the first: Amelia Thomson-Deveaux, "It Took a Long Time for Republicans to Abandon Nixon," FiveThirtyEight, October 9, 2019, https://fivethirtyeight.com/features/it-took-a-long-time-for-republicans-to-abandon-nixon/.

138   *Until its final hours:* Laurence Tribe and Joshua Matz, *To End a Presidency: The Power of Impeachment,* p. 143.

While public support: Ibid.

Now the governor of Maryland: Abbey Marshall, "Larry Hogan comes out in support of Trump impeachment inquiry," *Politico,* October 11, 2019, https://www.politico.com/news/2019/10/11/larry-hogan-trump-impeachment-044378.

5. Out of Many, One

140   "*Try to impeach him. Just try it*": *Roger Stone Says Impeach Trump, Get Ready for Civil War | TMZ,* 2017, https://www.youtube.com/watch?v=8hFRLbFaJEw.

Roger Stone, President Trump's: Cristiano Lima, "Roger Stone Predicts Violent 'insurrection' If Trump Is Impeached," *Politico,* August 24, 2017, https://www.politico.com/story/2017/08/24/roger-stone-predicts-insurrection-trump-impeachment-242010.

On September 29, 2019: "Donald J. Trump on Twitter: ". . . If the Democrats Are Successful in Removing the President from Office (Which They Will Never Be), It Will Cause a Civil War like Fracture in This Nation from Which Our Country Will Never Heal." Pastor Robert Jeffress, @FoxNews"," Twitter, September 29, 2019, https://twitter.com/realdonaldtrump/status/1178477539653771264.

Trump's supporters, however: Mary B. McCord. "Armed Militias Are Taking Trump's Civil War Tweets Seriously," *Lawfare,* October 2, 2019, https://www.lawfareblog.com/armed-militias-are-taking-trumps-civil-war-tweets-seriously.

141   *This wasn't necessarily:* "Oath Keepers," *Oath Keepers* (blog), December 13, 2018, https://oathkeepers.org/.

   As Jelani Cobb wrote: Jelani Cobb, "Why Trump, Facing Impeachment, Warns of Civil War," *The New Yorker,* October 5, 2019, https://www.newyorker.com/news/daily-comment/why-trump-facing-impeachment-warns-of-civil-war.

   As Martin Luther King, Jr., said in Memphis, Tennessee: "Here Is the Speech Martin Luther King Jr. Gave the Night before He Died," CNN, April 4, 2018, https://www.cnn.com/2018/04/04/us/martin-luther-king-jr-mountaintop-speech-trnd/index.html.

143   *because under existing law:* Zoe Tillman, "The Justice Department Said Trump's Ukraine Call Lacked A Thing 'Of Value.' Prosecutors Have Charged People Over Intangibles Before.," *BuzzFeed News,* October 3, 2019, https://www.buzzfeed news.com/article/zoetillman/justice-department-trump-call-ukraine-thing-value.

144   *As its chairman, Ellen Weintraub:* Weintraub, Ellen, *Twitter,* September 26, 2019, https://twitter.com/ellenlweintraub/status/1177335224662921226?lang=en.

   Elaborating on this point: Rupar, "America's top election official explains why Trump may be committing crimes," *Vox,* October 4, 2019, https://www.vox.com/2019/10/4/20898491/trump-foreign-solicitation-ukraine-china-fec-ellen-weintraub.

   The president's lawyer Jay Sekulow: "TheBeat w/Ari Melber on Twitter: '.@JaySeku-low on Trump's Ukraine Plot: "There's Nothing There That Rises to a Level of an Impeachable Offense." Https://T.Co/XQ0qxctgrJ' / Twitter," Twitter, accessed October 25, 2019, https://twitter.com/thebeatwithari/status/1181340451741278209.

   Turns out, Mueller said the opposite: Mueller report, p. 187.

149   *As Walter Dellinger:* Walter Dellinger, "Should we be able to indict a sitting president? Consider Spiro Agnew," *Washington Post,* December 16, 2018, https://www.washingtonpost.com/opinions/should-we-be-able-to-indict-a-sitting-president-consider-spiro-agnew/2018/12/16/6f88b6ce-ffcf-11e8-862a-b6a6f3ce8199_story.html.

150   *I'm heartened by the fact that:* "Can a President Be Indicted?," *CBS News,* May 29, 2018, https://www.cbsnews.com/news/can-a-president-be-indicted/.

   When Attorney General Jeff Sessions: Mueller Report.

151   *Since being appointed:* Julia Ainsley. "Attorney General William Barr Will Not Recuse Himself from Overseeing Mueller Probe." *NBC News,* March 5, 2019. https://www.nbcnews.com/politics/justice-department/attorney-general-william-barr-will-not-recuse-himself-overseeing-mueller-n979396.

   This is a clear case: Statement of New York City Bar, Oct. 23, 2019, available at https://www.nycbar.org/media-listing/media/detail/attorney-general-barr-should-recuse-himself-from-department-of-justice-review-of-ukraine-matter.

153   *And we know:* Kevin Liptak, Daniella Diaz, and Sophie Tatum, "Trump Pardons Former Sheriff Joe Arpaio—CNNPolitics," *CNN Politics,* August 27, 2017,

https://www.cnn.com/2017/08/25/politics/sheriff-joe-arpaio-donald-trump-pardon/index.html; Daniel Victor, "A Look at Dinesh D'Souza, Pardoned by Trump —The New York Times," *New York Times,* May 31, 2018, https://www.nytimes.com/2018/05/31/us/politics/dinesh-dsouza-facts-history.html.

155 *Our founders understood:* Madison, *Federalist No. 48,* February 1, 1788, https://avalon.law.yale.edu/18th_century/fed48.asp.